From a Milking Stool to the White House

My Life
by Harold Kneeland

PublishAmerica
Baltimore

First printing

PublishAmerica has allowed this work to remain exactly as the author intended, verbatim, without editorial input.

Hardcover 978-1-4489-6647-9
Softcover 978-1-4489-8378-0
PUBLISHED BY PUBLISHAMERICA, LLLP
www.publishamerica.com
Baltimore

Printed in the United States of America

Acknowledgment Statement

I am ever so grateful to the many people who have assisted and guided me on the road of life. I want to pay special thanks to my parents for their love and support in meeting the many challenges I encountered in my early years. I also want to express my appreciation and acknowledge my deceased wife's encouragement and financial contribution through her employment during my five and a half years of college while living in a 21 foot trailer. Deserving of special tribute, and critical to my initiation and completion of this book, was the encouragement I continually received from my daughter to write down my lifetime accomplishments so that she and my son would be able to tell their children and grandchildren the lifetime accomplishments of their grandfather. A special thanks is also in order to Donna, my significant other, for her expertise in the typing and computerizing this total book, and equally important, her patience in reading and rereading and listening to me read and reread the many paragraphs incorporated in this book for grammatical correctness, readability and consistency.

THE EARLY DAYS

During the early morning hours of July 31,1932 in the Johnson Memorial Hospital, Stafford Springs, Connecticut, Harold Eugene Kneeland was born to Mary Alice Kneeland (nee Thompson) and Harold Dewey Kneeland. I understand I was slightly ahead of my time as my parents were married on April 5th of that year, but I was anxious to get started on what was to become a very full and exciting life of **LOVE, CHALLENGES** and **ACHIEVEMENTS!**

It was a GREAT day!! I was born a Leo and have spent my life striving to meet the expectations of those born under this astrological sign…compassionate, generous and a demonstrative leader. What a challenge! Notwithstanding, the consensus of views expressed by visitors to my crib assured me that I had all the arrogant traits necessary to become an outstanding Leo!

After a brief exposure to life on the "outside," my mom and dad took me to our home in Storrs, Connecticut. Little did I know then that in a few short years I would have to share my parents and my home with 4 siblings; 2 brothers and 2 sisters.

Bill was born on August 6, 1933, Jacky on August 7, 1935, Wayne on July 3, 1936, and Sherrell was born on August 24, 1939.

Jacky and I are the only 2 family members still living. My mom died of an aortic aneurysm on August 28, 1982 at age 68; my dad died of a stroke on October 29, 1990 at age 79; Sherrell died on February 6, 1983 at age 43 of cancer of the spine; Bill died on May 23, 1985 of a heart attack at age 52, and Wayne died on January 7, 2004 of lung cancer at age 68.

When I was born Storrs was home for the Connecticut Agricultural College which my dad attended. He was an employee there at the time of my birth, performing miscellaneous farm duties in support of the college's farming activities. He was paid $90.00 PER MONTH, plus our rent-free home which was owned by the State College. Although we were pretty short on funds, love and affection were abundant in our home!

Storrs has since become the state's flagship of higher learning with 13 schools and colleges at the main campus in Storrs, separate Schools of Law and Social Work in Hartford, five regional campuses throughout the state and Schools of Medicine and Dentistry at the UConn Health Center in Farmington. The University serves more than 25,000 men and women on campuses throughout the state.

During my early years I used to accompany my parents to Pete Sabin's General Store where we purchased our groceries. Pete was in his sixties and sold groceries, fresh meats, shoes, boots, coveralls, bags of grain for animals, etc. He also kept several different types of "cold cuts" on the foot of his bed. To my knowledge no one ever got seriously sick from food poisoning from the lack of refrigeration. My dad had a "running tab" with Pete and at the end of each month he would take his check to Pete who would cash it, taking out what my father owed him for the month and giving my dad what was left which was usually less than $10.00. I can remember that my dad would often shake his head after Pete gave him back his change.

To supplement his income during the winter months, my dad used to trap skunks and muskrats, and hunt skunks at night in a pig lot near our house that had a concrete pad where garbage from the University dining hall was dumped daily. I used to go with him some nights and we would often find 2 to 6 skunks eating garbage on the concrete platform. Skunks are not scared easily and my dad used to walk right up to them, hit them once with a club killing them instantly. Yes, he would get a good spraying once in awhile from a skunk. My dad wore the same "skunk clothes" each night he hunted skunks, which was about once or twice a week

We also set traps to catch skunks around several chicken coops at the poultry plant near our home. We set a few traps for muskrats in a small stream near the house, but caught very few. My dad fixed a wire mesh platform between the front bumper of the car and the radiator grill, and if my mom came upon a dead skunk in the roadway that wasn't "squashed," she would take a metal hook that my dad had made and pick the skunk up and put it on the wire mesh and bring it home. My mom hated doing this so if any of us kids were in the car at the time we got to pick up the skunk and put it on the mesh platform.

My dad would skin the skunks or muskrats and stretch their skins over wooden forms that he had made until the pelts were cured. Once he had 10 or 15 pelts that were cured we used to sell them to a fur dealer who lived about 5 miles from our house. We kids used to go with him as we were all so excited to see how much money the dealer would give him for the furs.

My father also milked 2 cows every morning and evening that belonged to Dan Graf, his boss. He walked about a half mile to and from the cow barn every morning and evening, milked the cows, strained the milk, washed the milk pails and strainer etc and we got the milk from the evening milking and his boss got the morning milk. With 5 kids no milk was ever wasted.

We had a pet English Setter dog named Lobo who always accompanied my dad when he went to milk the cows. One night my dad had left for the barn and Lobo did not see him until he had already crossed the road in front of our house. Well, Lobo dashed across the street to catch up with my dad and was killed by a passing car. Needless to say, the whole family was very saddened by our loss. We gathered around my dad as he buried Lobo in a sheet-lined box in a corner of our garden.

We used to visit our paternal grandparents about every other Sunday. My maternal grandmother lived with us and my maternal grandfather died before we were born.

My dad's parents lived in Lebanon which was about 20 miles from our house. My Grampa often gave us a live chicken to take home with us. The chicken was always in a burlap bag and we kids would fight on our way home over who would hold the bag with the chicken.

During one of our trips home, Wayne, my youngest brother, and I were fighting in the back seat about holding the bag with the chicken. I finally opened the car door and pushed him out of the moving car. I looked back and Wayne was just getting up off the pavement and running up the road toward us. My dad, who never drove very fast (our cars were in such poor mechanical condition they barely ran at all) stopped and backed up to where Wayne was standing on the edge of the road. Wayne got into the car crying but did not appear to have any serious injuries. This was confirmed in a phone call to Dr. Gilman when we got home who instructed my mom to watch him closely and if he started vomiting, which he didn't, to call him. As for me, I was lectured by both my dad and my mom, and placed on probation for life!

Since I mentioned the condition of our cars, I want to take just a minute to say that they were so old and in such poor condition that I used to have my mom drop me off a block or two away from my friends' houses when I visited them. It was so embarrassing, especially when she dropped me off in front of my girl friend's house.

HURRICANE ARRIVES

On the morning of September 21, 1938, we woke up to a bright orange sky, the first sign of a very dangerous hurricane that was predicted to make land fall along the southern coast of Connecticut. By noon the winds were at hurricane strength and there were upwards of 50 dead chickens piled up in our living room that had been blown through our living room window

The UConn Archives of the storm reported that 22 of 26 hen houses were leveled and 200 hens were killed. A total of 1762 trees were cataloged as damaged or destroyed on campus. A huge maple tree on the edge of our front lawn was uprooted blocking all traffic on the main road to and from the north end of campus. The chimney on our house (we shared a 2 family duplex) was also blown over, crashing through our neighbor's roof and landing in their kitchen.

Shortly after noon I looked out through our broken living room window to see my dad and a co-worker with their arms locked around each other, struggling to stay on their feet as they approached our house. There was no loss of life or serious injuries recorded on campus. However, hundreds of lives were lost and thousands were injured throughout the Northeast due to the storm. The estimated cost in 1938 dollars for damage to dormitories, barns, and other campus property was $87,065.00 excluding trees and nearly $250,000 including trees. The storm began to subside over Storrs during the afternoon and my dad and others walked through the neighborhood looking for and assisting those in need of help.

LET THE FUN BEGIN

I was very lucky that our house was next to the University of Connecticut barn that housed about 25 Angus and Hereford cows and about 100 sheep divided pretty evenly between Dorsets, Shropshires and Southdowns. (This barn also required extensive repair following the hurricane.) Joe Pritchard, a great guy and second father to me, was the herdsman/shepherd for these animals.

Joe was born in England and immigrated to the United States aboard a ship transporting sheep from England to the U.S when he was 18 years old. When I got to be about 4 or 5 years old, Joe, with my parents consent, allowed me to help him with the barn chores…feeding and watering the animals, cleaning stalls, etc. My reward, after I became a 4-H Club member in 1940, was a FREE lamb each year for my 4-H Club project.

4-H CLUB

I joined the 4-H Club when I was 8 years old and remained an active member for 5 years. Each spring Joe would select the best Southdown lamb in the flock and give it to me for my 4-H project. I was then responsible for caring for the lamb including feeding, grooming and showing it at about five 4-H county fairs during the summer months.

The last fair of the season was a "biggie," the Eastern States Exposition held in Springfield, Mass. The Exposition was always held in September and lasted about 10 days. Mac, the name of my last 4-H Club lamb, was judged the Grand Champion lamb in the class of 4-H lambs in the Exposition in 1944. It was both a VERY HAPPY DAY and a VERY SAD DAY. Following the last show of the year, all the lambs were auctioned off to various retail meat dealers and grocery stores. They say big boys don't cry, but we sure did that day. Nobody had to draw me a picture of what was going to happen to them once we handed them over to the buyer.

CUB SCOUTS/BOY SCOUTS

When I was 9 years old I joined the Cub Scouts and became a member of Mrs. Kinsey's Den. Mrs. Kinsey was a great den mother and also the mother of one of my best grammar school friends, Phil Kinsey. A year later my brother Bill also joined our den. I remained in the Cub Scouts for 3 years, achieving the rank of Webelo and was then promoted into the Storrs Troop of the Boy Scouts of America at age 12.

I went to Boy Scout camp the first summer and was homesick from the time my folks drove out of the camp until they returned to pick me up one week later...that was the end of my going to scout camp, although I thoroughly enjoyed our week-end hikes and overnight camp outs. I reached the rank of Life Scout, lacking only 4 of the required 24 merit badges to have become an Eagle Scout. However, I was 15 at the time and working, was a Freshman in high school, and simply did not have the time necessary to keep up with scouting activities.

THE SCHOOL YEARS

I attended the Storrs Grammar School beginning in the fall of 1938 when I was 6 years old and delivered the commencement address as president of our graduating class 8 years later in 1946. When I first started grammar school I was scared to mingle with the kids in my class so my mother drove me to school each day and I would sit in the car in the parking lot until the school bell rang and then run into my classroom.

Once I got rid of my shyness (about 2 weeks) I really enjoyed school and the teachers as well, especially my 8th grade teacher, Mrs. Lillian Custer, a beautiful, sexy, 23 year old redhead. She and her husband Bob, a B-24 Bomber pilot during World War II and at that time a graduate student at Uconn studying for his PHD in chemistry, used to take us on nature hikes, fishing in local rivers, ball games, etc during vacations and on weekends. We really enjoyed the extra-curricular activities that they planned and shared with us during our last year in the Storrs Grammar School.

I should mention that my dad helped me write my grammar school graduation speech, the first line of which I have never forgotten… "It is with a slight feeling of sadness and bewilderment that our years at the Storrs Grammar School have come to an end." Those few words expressed the feelings of the whole class, all 13 of us.

MY HIGH SCHOOL YEARS

Following graduation from grammar school I started a part-time job milking cows from 5:00 to 7:00 AM and 4:30 to 6:30 PM, 7 days a week at a farm that was about a mile from my house. I had to get a job in order to buy the school clothes and shoes that I wanted for high school. My primary transportation was a bicycle except in very cold or inclement weather when my mom would take me and pick me up. I worked at this job for about a year before going to work in the Nutmeg Fountain, a very popular college student hangout for hamburgers, subs, ice cream sundaes, etc. I worked evenings and weekends at the Nutmeg the last 3 years of high school.

During my 2nd year in high school I bought a 124 base accordion and took lessons from Mrs. Nancy Hall for about 2 years. It was a bit inconvenient as I had to get off the school bus and walk about a half-mile to her house carrying my accordion, books, etc. Nevertheless, it was a great experience and although I never became a "concert" accordionist I enjoyed playing at various outings, Grange meetings, parties, and the Wittlesbach Hotel in Oberammergau, Germany. (more on that later)

OK…let's get back to my high school days!! As there was no high school in Storrs, I had to take a 12 mile bus ride daily to attend Windham High School in Willimantic. I started high school in the Fall of 1946, graduating in June 1950. Because I had to take the bus to and from high school, plus my work schedule, I was unable to participate in many of the school athletic programs. However, I did play 2nd base on the Storrs Wildcats baseball team during my summer vacations which I really enjoyed. The team was made up of high school kids from Storrs and we played teams from neighboring towns.

I got my driver's license when I was 16 which allowed me greater freedom to be with my school friends on weekends and during vacations. Unfortunately, the first evening that I went out in my dad's car after getting my driver's license I hit a parked car on a narrow street in Willimantic while lighting a cigar. The crash dented the right front fender on my dad's car (but it was still drivable) and the left rear fender of the parked car. It was at night and no one was around so I stuck a note under the windshield wipers with my name and phone number. My friends and I then took off immediately looking for a service station, garage, or any other place that we hoped might be able to repair my dad's car before I had to take it home. It was a waste of time!!

When I got home, about 5:00 AM, my dad was still in bed, but it wasn't long before he bounded into my room wanting to know what the hell I had hit. I told him that I was "blinded" by oncoming headlights on Jackson St. in Willimantic and hit a parked car. (I only lied when I absolutely had to, and this was one of those rare occasions when I had to). After explaining that I had left my name and phone number on a note under the windshield wipers of the other car, the "aggravation level" gradually subsided. Fortunately, that was the only accident I ever had with my dad's car.

My sweetheart during my early high school years was Joyce Segar. Soon after graduation from high school, Joyce married a student who was in the class ahead of us. In about 1996 my sister Jacky received a call from Joyce's younger sister saying that Joyce was dying of ovarian cancer in the Infants and Women's Hospital in Providence, Rhode Island, and she had asked her to try to contact me through my sister and ask if I could possibly visit her. I never hesitated a minute to make travel plans from Waverly, Ohio, where I was employed at the time by Lockheed Martin, to Providence.

Once my travel plans were finalized I called Joyce to tell her I was on my way and when I would arrive at the hospital. When I arrived there a day or two later, the nurses had bought her a wig and applied lipstick, make-up, etc. Needless to say it was a very emotional reunion. After visiting with her for 3 days I left to return to Ohio...Joyce died about a month later.

I graduated from high school in June 1950. Since I was not in the upper 25 percentile of my graduating class, I had to take an entrance exam in order to enroll as an undergraduate student at the University of Connecticut (Uconn). I took the exam and failed it. Since I had to wait 6 months before I could take it again, I got a job as a fireman with the UConn Security Department. I had spent a lot of my free time during my high school years at the security office doing a variety of jobs including answering phone calls, going out on patrol with some of the security officers, assisting on ambulance runs, etc.

When I talk about the security office, I can't help recalling the evening when Tom McGrath, one of the police officers, offered to sell me a Winchester Model 94 30-30 deer rifle for $10.00. I bought it in a heartbeat! He also threw in several 30-30 shells with the rifle. I was probably 16 or 17 at the time. I immediately got in touch with Phil Kinsey, one of my close school friends and we went out and purchased a 5-cell flashlight. We were now ready to go out "jack lighting deer." It was about midnight when we decided to check out Kessel's apple orchard which was about a half-mile from my house. We lived across the street from the Kessels and knew them well. In fact, I went to school with one of their daughters.

Phil and I decided that their orchard was the place to go, especially since there were no houses near the orchard, and there was a cart path that went past the back side of the orchard. I parked my dad's car in a secluded area not far from the cart path, loaded the shells into the rifle and Phil and I started walking down the path about 75 yards from the edge of the orchard. Shortly after we began our walk Phil turned the flashlight on in the direction of the orchard. WOW! We saw 3 pairs of eyes loping slowly in an open field along the edge of the orchard.

I braced myself against a tree and started following the last pair of eyes that kept reflecting in and out of the flashlight beam. I was aiming the rifle at an area about 3 feet behind and on the same plane as the deer's eyes. Aiming slightly above the deer's body would compensate for my suspicion that he was slightly out of range for a 30-30 carbine. Suddenly his eyes reflected into the light beam and I fired!! Being the middle of the night and with no background noise, it sounded like a cannon had gone off. Phil and I took off running to find the deer. We looked everywhere and could find nothing. I wasn't too terribly surprised under the circumstances. We went back to the car and went home for the night.

The next day I kept thinking I should ride my bike down the cart path and check to see if there might be a dead deer in the field adjacent to the orchard. THERE HE WAS…an 8 point buck lying right where I thought he should be, even though we could not find him in the dark. I had hit him just behind the right shoulder and he must have dropped in his tracks.

I knew my dad would be furious, but I had to tell him so we could move the deer before someone spotted it, if they hadn't already. (Apparently no one had.) When I went home I told my mom the whole story. Her first comment was, "Why did you do it? You know your father is going to be very upset." Well, dad wasn't home then, but when he came in my mother told him that WE had to talk to him. Before she could even tell him the whole story he was livid…reminding me that hunting deer in Connecticut was illegal (I knew that), jack-lighting deer was a felony (I didn't know that), hunting deer on state property (the deer was killed on state property) was subject to a fine of $500 or more (I didn't know that) and since he was employed by the state he could be fired (I didn't know that).

By now the expletives were flying! I was afraid he would ask me for the rifle and then shoot me with it (not really). I disappeared for a while and by the time dinner was ready he was asking me what are WE going to do with the deer. We decided to carry the deer to a shelter behind horse barn hill where horses pastured out for the winter could get shelter from snow storms, high winds, etc. This shelter was a good ¼ mile from where the deer lay, and involved crossing through rough terrain, including a 5 foot wall and a 6 foot perimeter fence.

I was told that I would dig a hole outside the shelter where everything would be buried except the meat which we would take home…it sounded OK, but I had hoped to keep the head, (the deer's head that is, not mine) and have it mounted. When it got dark my dad and I, equipped with a lantern, a flashlight, a long wooden pole, ropes, knives, a shovel, etc. left home to carry the deer to the horse shelter. After tying the deer's feet together around the pole we tried to lift it up. I couldn't carry my end of the pole (the back end). We tried everything to move the deer, all to no avail.

We would have to go to our neighbor, Gil Farrington, and ask if he would be willing to help us move the deer for ½ of the meat.

Gil jumped at the opportunity. All 3 of us returned to the deer, moved it to the horse shelter, dressed it, buried the head, skin, guts, etc. in the hole I had dug and then camouflaged. Altogether it took about 2 hours to do everything, including dressing the deer into 4 quarters. When we finally got home, dad had cooled down a bit, and when we started eating venison instead of fried boloney he started to smile again. Needless to say, my deer hunting days were over! I sold my rifle to avoid any temptation to repeat what I had just been through.

NOVEMBER 11, 1950... A DAY WE WILL NEVER FORGET

It was my dad's 40th birthday, and he was called to his mom's house early that morning to join his family who had gathered to be with his mom who was dying of breast cancer—she died late that afternoon. I was working at the firehouse when a fire call came in about noon that the house we lived in was on fire. By the time we got to the house it was engulfed in flames. The fire had started in the attic of the family who shared our duplex house with us. We were able to save some furniture and some clothes.

I called my dad at his mom's house to tell him of the fire. He and my mom returned to our house and started calling friends to see where we might stay until they were able to find temporary housing for us. I moved in with Jack and Ginny Francois...Jack was a Uconn security officer. My brother Bill moved in with the Warren family...he and their son Charles played guitars on various occasions in the Storrs area. My 2 sisters stayed with a great aunt and Wayne and my parents stayed with my mother's aunt. As I recall, temporary housing for our whole family was arranged during the next few weeks in a 3 bedroom apartment.

COLLEGE ENTRANCE EXAM... DECISION TIME...

Now, back to my college entrance exam...I took it again in early December 1950 and failed it again. At that point I decided it was time to do my duty to God and Country as the Korean War had just started a few months earlier. One of my high school classmates, decided he would enlist with me. We started with the Navy recruiter who gave us little encouragement that we would go through boot training together, but did indicate that I would be able to attend about any school of my choice following 6 weeks of boot camp...However, since we would not be together long, we went to the Army recruiter who didn't give us any encouragement either, but we decided to enlist in the Army anyway. A week or so later we got our notice to report to the Army recruitment center in Hartford, Connecticut.

We spent 2 days at the recruitment center beginning at 6:00 AM, taking aptitude tests, physical exams, etc. The third day (January 15th) we were to be at the Center at 6:00 AM for final processing and to be sworn into the Army. Following the swearing in we would then be given an overnight pass with orders to report to the Center at 6:00 AM the next morning to board a bus that would take us to Camp Devens in northern

Massachusetts. When I stopped at my friend's house to pick him up on the 15th to drive us to the Recruitment Center his mother answered the door and told me that he wasn't going...he was thinking about joining the National Guard instead.

I was shocked and disappointed, but I wasn't about to back out. I went to Hartford alone and was sworn in. My mom and dad drove me to the Recruitment Center the next morning. I boarded the bus and as we pulled away from the curb I saw my mom crying in my dad's arms. There are no words to express how I felt at that moment!

YOU'RE IN THE ARMY NOW!!

Upon arrival at Camp Devens that afternoon, we were marched to a barracks that was empty except for a line of steel beds with mattresses along each wall. We were then issued bedding and taught how to make the bed, military style. Later that afternoon we were marched to the barber shop where we were "buzzed" in about 2 minutes. Upon returning to the barracks we were told that most of us would be transferred within the next couple of weeks to military bases elsewhere in the U.S. to begin basic training. In the interim, our daily schedule would begin by getting up at 4:00 AM, mess (breakfast) at 4:30A.M. and to be in formation in front of the barracks at 6:00 A.M. to be briefed on activities scheduled for the day, including orientations/exercises on military practices and procedures, issuance of military clothes and shoes, aptitude tests, marching exercises, saluting, etc.

I had my first baptism to military discipline my first night. At 20 hours (8:00 PM) a member of the base cadre, referred to as the CQ (Charge of Quarters) came through the barracks announcing that he was turning off the lights and they were NOT to be turned on again until he turned them on at 0400 hours (4:00 AM) in the morning. About five minutes later the lights came on and the CQ returned, advising that he was going to turn off the lights one more time and if they came on again appropriate action would be taken. He turned the lights off and within five minutes the lights came on again!

The CQ returned and ordered all of us in the barracks (about 30 in all) to get dressed and line up outside the barracks or face disciplinary action for disobeying a direct order. He had our attention and we assembled outside the barracks, a bitter cold night with at least a foot of snow on the ground. To make it worse, the only clothes and shoes we had were those we wore to camp earlier that day as we had not yet been issued any military clothing or shoes.

We assembled outside and he ordered us to start marching in single file around the perimeter of the barracks and he said he would monitor us from inside the building. He did say that we would be allowed a ten minute break every hour on the hour to come inside the barracks, and that this exercise would continue until 4:00 AM.

During our 10 minute break at midnight, the CQ advised that we would be excused from further marching, expressing the hope that we had learned a lesson in military discipline. I had, and hopefully the draftee from Queens, New York, by the name of Wheelock, who allegedly was responsible for turning the lights on in violation of the CQ's order, had learned his lesson too. Hopefully he had!

During our morning briefing we received our military serial numbers; mine was RA 11217832. With few exceptions most of the serial numbers began with "US," meaning that the individual had been drafted into the Army. I was among the very few whose serial number began with "RA" which stood for Regular Army. I was proud of this distinction, even though it was interpreted by most to mean "Real Asshole."

By mid-week I was told that I would be transferred to Camp

Picket, Virginia, for basic training, probably during the following week. I was happy as that was a lot closer to Connecticut than bases located in Georgia or Texas where most of the recruits were to be assigned for their basic training.

I immediately called home to see if my folks would be able to visit me that weekend as it would be my last chance to be with them until I completed my 16 weeks of basic training. Of course they did, arriving about noon on Sunday. Of all days, I was put on KP that Sunday morning. Although I got word about noon that my parents had arrived at the visitors' center, I was told by the mess sargeant that I had to remain in the mess hall until 3:30 PM.

When I got off duty I had to go to my barracks and change into my class "A" uniform in order to get into the visitors' center. It was close to 4:30 before I got to visit with my family, and the Visitors' Center closed at 6:00 PM. I was so happy to see them, even for a short time, but saying goodbye again was extremely difficult knowing that I would not be seeing them again until I completed basic training, about 4 months into the future.

ON TO CAMP PICKETT, VIRGINIA

Our trip to Camp Pickett began on Thursday, February 1, 1951. We packed what belongings we had into a duffle bag and boarded a truck that took us to a railroad siding where railroad coach cars, not Pullmans, were lined up to take us to Camp Pickett. I don't know how many railroad cars were on the siding or how many troops boarded the train. I remember there were more railroad cars than I could count when I arrived at the siding and I saw several truck loads of soldiers arriving to board the train.

As I remember, we left the siding in the early evening and didn't arrive at Camp Pickett until Sunday afternoon. As you might have surmised, substantially more time was spent sitting on railroad "sidings" watching trains go by versus time spent actually traveling. Meals were distributed in lunch bags/ boxes throughout the trip. Our train seats served as our sleeping accommodations as well.

Upon arrival at Camp Pickett we were greeted by a Colonel. I believe he was the Commanding Officer of the 169th Infantry Regiment of the 43rd Infantry Division. We marched to a nearby parade field and stood in a cold drizzly rain for about 30 minutes while the Colonel lectured us on what we were and what we would be when he finished training us. His tirade went something like this…"You're soldiers, you're shit, you're nothing but a bunch of bowery bums, but when I get through with you, you'll be soldiers." After about 30 minutes of that we were marched to our company areas…I was assigned to "G" Company, 169th Infantry Regiment.

I was very fortunate to have been assigned to the 43rd Infantry Division as it was also the Connecticut State National Guard unit prior to its activation on September 5, 1950. Within an hour or so from the time I got to my company area, I located an uncle, Roland Marshall, a Sargeant with the 169th Infantry Regiment. He and my Aunt Julia lived in a rented apartment in Blackistone, Va, about 5 miles from the base. He immediately insisted on taking me to their apartment in the trunk of his car. I told him absolutely not! I was too afraid I would be caught and my military career would start in the stockade. He convinced me that he would not suggest doing anything that could cause me a problem and with that we were off!

I spent a couple hours having dinner with him and my aunt before returning to the base. Upon arrival back in my company area I discovered that bed assignments mattresses, blankets, etc. had been issued to all new arrivals during my absence. Fortunately, I found someone in the company supply organization who helped me get a bed assignment on the second floor of the barracks and issued me the bedding supplies I needed. I took a shower, the first in several days, and went to bed.

Our schedule, when we weren't on bivouac at one of the several training areas, was to be up by 6:00 AM, breakfast at 6:30 and assemble in formation in the company area at 8:00.AM for assignments/orders of the day, etc. The first week or so was devoted primarily to orientations on our training curriculum. We were informed that we were assigned to the 169th Infantry

Regiment for basic training as infantry soldiers and upon completion of training would be reassigned to a Korean Casualty Replacement Battalion. We were also issued the balance of clothing, shoes, etc. that we didn't receive at Camp Devens, plus M-1 rifles, back backs, helmets, water canteens, etc.

The first weeks of our basic training were spent learning the detailed nomenclature of the M-1 rifle (adequate to disassemble and re-assemble all basic parts in the dark), live firing on the rifle range, arming and throwing live hand grenades, learning the nomenclature and firing 30 caliber machine guns, crawling through the infiltration course with live 30 caliber machine gun bullets being fired over our heads (30 inches above ground level) during day and night exercises, moving over open, rough terrain while under the cover of exploding artillery fire and general offensive and defensive maneuvers under simulated combat conditions with an aggressor force participating as the enemy.

The above training activities/exercises were conducted in various training areas within the Camp Picket military reservation. My training schedule was interrupted after the first 3 weeks of basic training because of illness. I went on sick call on a Monday morning and every morning during the remainder of that week, with a chest cold and fever. Each day I was sent back to my company area with a medical slip recommending "light duty." These slips were ignored.

The First Sargeant put me on KP duty beginning at 3:00 AM every other day and cleaning 30 caliber machine guns on alternating days. On Saturday I was coughing up blood, nauseated and could no longer walk to sick bay, about 4 blocks from my barracks. One of my friends went to sick bay for me and told a medic that I was in bed in my barracks and could not walk to the medical facility. The medic came back to the barracks with my friend and took my temperature which was 104.5 degrees! He left saying that one of the doctors would be back to examine me.

The doctor came about 2 hours later and concluded that I had lobar pneumonia and he would make arrangements for me to be taken to the 2nd Army Hospital on base. He gave me a note to give to the admission's office upon arrival there. About an hour later, 2 medical corpsmen came upstairs, put me on a stretcher and took me down to the ambulance. They drove me to the hospital, stopping in front of the admission's office. At that point one of the corpsmen opened the sliding glass window at the rear of the cab and told me to lift the latch on the rear door and go on into the admission's office.

I entered the hospital in a state of shock, dressed only in my long johns and socks. I found myself in a waiting room full of dependents and children. I signed in at the waiting room window and gave the medic the note from the doctor. I was instructed to have a seat and someone would be with me as soon as possible.

After waiting about an hour, a medic came out and had me follow him to an examining room. The attending doctor concurred with the MD's note that I had brought with me…I had a severe case of lobar pneumonia. I was then given directions to Ward B-14 where I was to be admitted. It seemed as if I walked miles before I finally found Ward B-14. I opened the door to the ward and was immediately stopped by a Sargeant who said they were having an inspection and what did I want. I gave him the doctor's admission's slip and he told me to get in the latrine and be quiet!

Following the inspection I was assigned a bed and later that afternoon was examined by an MD. I was put on penicillin and assured that someone would be checking back with me later that afternoon. I have no recollection of anyone checking on me…in fact the next thing I knew it was Tuesday afternoon. I had gone into a coma. I found out later that I was placed on the critical list and the Red Cross was notified to contact my parents and advise them of my condition. I later learned that the Red Cross never made contact with my parents.

Shortly after treatment began, I learned from a very kind civilian nurse that the stinging I experienced after each penicillin shot was because I was being treated with crystalline penicillin and not procaine penicillin which was reserved for Korean veterans. Of 30 or so patients in the ward, about 25 were Korean War veterans who were being treated for frozen extremities, amputations in some cases, plus combat wounds. I had absolutely no problem with the veterans getting the procane penicillin; however, after a day or two I was no longer experiencing the stinging following my penicillin shots. The next time she came in to give me a shot I smiled and she smiled back. She went on to say that because of the frequency of my shots she had obtained permission to change them from crystalline to procaine penicillin. Throughout my 3 week stay in the hospital she took on the role of being my foster mom…she was so kind and considerate of all the patients' needs!

I dropped a short note to my girlfriend at the time, Jean Lincoln, telling her I was in the hospital. I did not share this with my mom as I didn't want to worry her. Well, Jean met my mom in the grocery store a few days later and asked her how I was doing. My mom responded to the effect that she had not heard from me in awhile as I was on maneuvers. At that point Jean let the cat out of the bag, telling her that she had received a short note from me and that I was in the hospital with pneumonia. Well, my folks contacted Julia and Roland and they called the hospital, confirming that I was a patient. Julia informed my mom and the next day they were on their way to Camp Pickett to visit me. They remained about a week and I am sure their visit hastened my recovery.

I was in the hospital about 3 weeks and was discharged on a Sunday afternoon. I was really excited as I walked back to my barracks as I had been given a note signed by one of the hospital doctors to my First Sargeant, recommending that because of the severity of my illness I be given a 30 day convalescent leave. When I got back to the barracks I gave my First Sargeant the note and I couldn't believe it when he tore it up, saying that I was already behind in my basic training and there would be no leave.

By late March I was eligible to get week-end passes from noon Saturday until 6:00 AM Monday, subject of course to my having passed the Saturday 10:00 AM inspection which usually lasted about an hour and which I didn't always pass. We were encouraged to take advantage of every opportunity to go home as we were vulnerable to being placed on orders for Korea at any time.

Traveling from Camp Pickett to Connecticut and to return within the allowed 42 hours was very trying! It started at 12 noon departing camp in a limousine with 9 others at a cost of $10.00 each from Camp Pickett to Washington, D.C., about a 4 hour ride. There was a train that left D.C for Penn Station, New York City at about 4:30 PM which I didn't always catch because of the "tight" time constraints.

Once in New York City, I had about 30 minutes to get from Penn Station to Grand Central Station in order to connect with the Montreal Express that departed Grand Central around 10:00 PM, arriving in Hartford, Conn. about 1:00 AM. My mom and dad would pick me up and we would head for home, about a 25-30 mile drive. After a brief chit-chat it was to bed and up about 7:00 AM.

The morning consisted of a visit with family, and occasionally going to church. I had to be in Hartford at about 1:30 PM to catch a train that went through to Washington, D.C., arriving about

11:00 PM. Once in D.C., the hunt was on to find 6-8 soldiers to share the cab fare back to Camp Pickett. I was always successful in joining a group and arriving back at camp before the 6:00AM deadline.

On one occasion I was able to join 2 soldiers who were friends of the family who were driving from Willimantic, Connecticut back to Camp Pickett. We left Willimantic about 2:00 PM on a Sunday afternoon and had 3 flat tires along the way, arriving at Camp Pickett about 6:30 AM Monday. My punishment for being 30 minutes late was a 2 week restriction to the company area, KP on weekends and up to 28 hours (2 hours per day) extra duty during the 2 weeks restriction.

KOREA...YES THEN NO

In May I was told that I was on orders to go to Korea and I went home on a 7 day embarkation leave. Not wanting to upset my family, I told them that I was expecting to be shipped out soon, but did not know where. After enjoying the 7 days with family and friends, I boarded what I knew would be my last train ride between Hartford and D.C. for a long time. Scared yes, but proud to serve!!

Upon arrival back at Camp Pickett, I was told that I had been "scratched" from the orders as I had not completed the minimum 16 weeks of basic training required for transfer to a combat area...the 3 weeks I had spent in the hospital with lobar pneumonia made the difference!

A GOOF THAT COULD HAVE CHANGED MY LIFE

I learned from one of my friends that the 43rd Division Military Police Company was recruiting soldiers with prior police/ security experience. At my first opportunity (about a day later) I went to the MP Company and spoke with First Sargeant, Daniel Leone, who was from Hartford, Connecticut, the "home base" of the MP Company prior to the 43rd Infantry Division activation from National Guard to U.S. Army status in September, 1950.

My interview with Sargeant Leone went very well! After about 10 minutes he went into Captain John Carroll's office, the Company Commander at the time, to ask if he would want to interview me. Before he went into his office however, he told me that if the Captain wanted to speak with me to be sure to give him a "snappy" salute when I entered and left his office. Within a minute or two Sargeant Leone opened the door and invited me in, introducing me to Captain Carroll. I snapped to attention and gave him a salute he would never forget!

The Captain ordered me to be at ease, and I made the biggest military blunder of my career. When he ordered me to be at ease I relaxed my body, and I believe I even rested my hand on his desk. Upon being ordered "at ease" I should have immediately taken the "Parade Rest" position...spreading my feet a foot apart, snapping my hands together behind my back, standing in an erect position, head facing straight ahead.

I knew this, but before I could come to my senses the Captain "barked," "I said at ease. Do you know what that means?" While snapping to the proper position, I responded, "Yes, Sir, I apologize." After answering several questions regarding my responsibilities with the Univ. of Conn. Security Department, the Captain turned to Sargeant Leone and said something to the effect, "Let's give him a chance." As the sargeant opened the door to leave, I snapped to attention, saluted the Captain and said "Thank you, Sir!"

Once outside, Sargeant Leone gave me a good chewing-out, telling me how embarrassed he was and how surprised he was that the Captain hadn't dismissed me immediately. I acknowledged and apologized for the goof. There was no excuse. I assured him it would not happen again and that I was looking forward to becoming a Military Policeman in his company. The only thing I can say in my defense, if there is any defense at all, is that this was the first time I had ever been engaged, one-on-one, in conversation with an officer.

THE CHALLENGES OF A MILITARY POLICEMAN

In early May, I received orders transferring me from the 169th Infantry Regiment to the 43rd Military Police Company. I was ELATED!! Staff Sargeant "Red" Menard was my squad leader and coach in learning the responsibilities of an MP…I could not have had a better instructor or friend than he. We hit it off from the very start.

The first weeks were spent primarily on how to ride a motorcycle, doing guard duty at ammunition dumps, gasoline storage areas and General's guard as assigned. General's guard was primarily guarding the residence of Major General Kenneth Cramer, Commanding General of the 43rd Infantry Division. His residence was under military police guard around the clock, with 2 guards during nighttime hours. What spare time I had was spent shining my leather uniform belts, holster, boots, etc until I could use them as a mirror.

I quickly gained experience and confidence in knowing what to do, primarily from "on the job" training. My duties began to take on new assignments, including guard duty at personnel and truck traffic entrances/exits to various military areas and facilities. Within a month I was accompanying some of the more senior MPs on weekend duty, patrolling the streets in neighboring cities to assure that the conduct of all military personnel on pass was in accordance with military standards and orders.

On occasion we were accompanied by a city policeman in the event civilians might be involved in any incidents involving military personnel. The decision as to whether you would be accompanied by a civilian policeman was often determined by the city/area you were patrolling.

During June and July the 43rd Infantry Division went on "Combat Readiness" maneuvers at AP Hill Military Reservation in Virginia. It was about 3 hours north of Camp Pickett. We worked in conjunction with both Civil and State Police, including town patrol, traffic control, operation of straggler lines and assisting in establishing and maintaining POW enclosures.

Those of us who had private cars were allowed to take them with us, which I did at the urging of "Red" Menard. About the third week into the maneuvers, "Red" told me that he and I, and another MP from Manchester, Conn. were going to drive my car to Connecticut that night...WOW! I couldn't believe what he was saying. We were deep into "aggressor forces" territory and he had already arranged for us to be picked up after dark by an MP patrol that would take us to my car parked off the reservation. It happened, and the 3 of us were on our way to Connecticut shortly after 8:00PM in my 1941 Chevrolet coup.

After a long night of alternating drivers, we dropped Menard off in Hartford about 9:00 AM and I went on to drop John Givens, our third passenger, off in Manchester. I then headed for Storrs arriving about 9:30AM, and surprising the hell out of my mom when she realized it was me who drove into the yard. I told her I had a 3-day pass and had driven up from AP Hill with Menard and another MP.

Two days later, after a brief but pleasant unexpected visit with my family, I left home, picked up John and Menard and headed back to AP Hill, arriving late that night. After parking the car near the entrance to AP Hill, we walked into the bivouac area until we came upon a jeep. With our MP armbands in place, we stopped the jeep and told the driver we had to be taken to the MP headquarters. After driving around attempting to locate the MP headquarters, we finally found it about dawn.

Prior to arriving at the MP Headquarters, Red instructed both John and me to listen to what he had to say to Sargeant Leone and to just agree with everything he said. As we drove up, Sargeant Leone asked, "Where the hell have you guys been?" I can remember it like it was yesterday as Menard responded to the effect, "Don't give us any shit, Dan. We were captured by the aggressor force 3 days ago, have been held under guard in their prisoner confinement area and have been given about 3 cans of "C" rations since we were captured. Red went on to ask where the hell were the MP patrols, indicating that we were ready to "make a run for it" as soon as we saw a friendly jeep.

I couldn't believe it…Sargeant Leone responded with a "no kidding," and told us to get cleaned up and he would have 3-day passes for the 3 of us when we were ready. We washed our faces and shaved, (only field showers were available when scheduled) got our passes and went to Colonial Beach, Virginia, for 3 days.

Shortly following our return from Colonial Beach, I was scheduled for 1 week of General's Guard duty back at Camp Pickett along with 5 other MPs. Schedules had already been worked out whereby one MP would be on duty between 6:00 AM and 12 noon, 1 MP from 12 noon to 6:00 PM, 2 MPs from 6:00 PM to midnight and 2 MPs from Midnight to 6:00AM. Being "low-man-on-the-totem-pole" I, along with Emil Daub, would be on the Midnight to 6:00 AM shift. Since General Cramer was spending most of his time at AP Hill, and according to the MPs whom we relieved, neither he nor his wife were at home during the week just ended while they were on duty.

Based upon this information, Emil and I decided to adopt the same "sleep schedule" as our predecessors, take turns sleeping 2 hours each between the hours of 1:00 AM and 5:00 AM, with both of us walking around the house during the first and last hour of our watch. Neither the General nor his wife came home during the first few days of the week.

On the last night of our guard duty, I believe it was a Saturday night, Emil's "sleep shift" was from 1:00AM to 3:00 AM. He went around the back of the house to take his nap and I sat in a hammock facing the driveway while he slept so that I would be certain to see any car that might turn into the driveway. Well, I had dozed off when suddenly headlight beams crossed the yard. I jumped up, ran around the house and got Emil up and we were both standing and saluting the General when his car stopped at the front door. He greeted us, and while standing at attention, we responded with, "Good evening, Sir!." It seemed at this point that he had not seen me asleep when they drove into the driveway.

We resumed our guard protocol, walking around the house in opposite directions. After 10 or 15 minutes I observed through the kitchen window that Mrs. Cramer had set the kitchen table with 4 cups and saucers and 4 cake plates. Being the ever optimistic individual that I am, I asked myself if we might be going to be invited in for coffee and cake. Of course NOT, I told myself. Well, about then I heard General Cramer call, "Boys, would you like a little snack?" I was closest to the door and answered "YES SIR" for both of us.

For once I had my wits about me and I informed the General that to assure his safety, I would continue walking my post while my partner joined him and Mrs. Cramer and I would join them as soon as my partner returned to his post. The General's immediate response was to the effect that that is the level of responsibility he expects from his soldiers but doesn't always find it among his officers or enlisted men. He took my name and stated that he would be informing Captain Carroll, my Company Commander, of my outstanding performance in this instance. WOW…what could have been a night when I was arrested for dereliction of duty and subsequent Court Martial, I really came out "smelling like a rose." I anxiously awaited a similar compliment from Captain Carroll, thinking that General Cramer would certainly have been in contact with him as he stated he would, but it was never forthcoming.

OPERATION SOUTHERN PINES... FORT BRAGG, NORTH CAROLINA

To culminate its stateside training, the 43rd Infantry Division, in August 1951, joined with the 28th Infantry Division, the 82nd Airborne Division and other supporting units in Exercise Southern Pine at Fort Bragg, North Carolina.

Working in conjunction with local and State Police, the 43rd Division Military Police Company provided traffic patrols and escort duty during the move from Camp Pickett, Va. to Southern Pines. I was one of several Military Police patrols leading and escorting 43rd Infantry Division convoys through Raleigh, North Carolina 24 hours per day. This assignment lasted approximately 10 days, during which time local citizens were continuously bringing us food and drink.

On August 15th the Division moved into an offensive position and the Military Police company began functioning as a combat unit, involving a variety of duties including traffic control points, patrols, establishing and maintaining POW enclosures, security of the Division Headquarters, etc. The efficiency and alertness of the MP company during the maneuvers was commended by prominent civilians and high ranking military officials observing the exercise.

With the termination of the maneuvers in late August, I was again assigned to lead and escort military convoys through Raleigh, North Carolina, enroute back to Camp Pickett. Va.

GERMANY BOUND

On October 10 the Military Police company moved out of Camp Pickett to join General Eisenhower's NATO Army. We boarded a fleet of buses to Hampton Roads, Va. Port of Embarkation, where we boarded the army transport ship, General M.B. Stewart.

Our quarters on E deck (4 levels below the main deck) were cramped to say the least, but I was "on board" early enough to secure the top "hammock" or "bunk" if you will, of 4 or 5 "hanging" hammocks. There were several rows of these "hanging" hammock units in the compartment, designated as Compartment E 4. Although my hammock was close to the ceiling, I preferred tolerating the heat and smell of puke from those suffering sea sickness versus getting any of it on me or my bed. That turned out to be a smart decision on my part!

The General M.B. Stewart headed out to sea about 4:00 PM on October 11th while the 2nd Army Band played "So Long, Its Been Good to Know You." The band had hardly stopped playing when the first signs of sea sickness became apparent. Fortunately for me, I have never experienced sea sickness or any other type of motion sickness. Seeing seasick sailors was quite a sight for us "ground pounders" who were not sick!!

Our mission aboard ship was to provide security guards for off limit areas. Practice boat drills also kept most of us who were not sea sick moving from various posts on deck.

About mid-way across the Atlantic we encountered a storm that some of the sailors were saying was the tail end of a hurricane. The storm caused many of those on board who had not been sea sick to join those who were. The ship's log for that day recorded "seas moderate, 40 foot swells." I would hate to be aboard a ship when the seas were rough, although I was not feeling sick from the high rolling swells. It was actually rather exciting to watch and experience the ship come off a high wave and in seconds be surrounded by water that was 40 feet above the ship.

CAMP Y-79...TENT CITY

On October 20 the White Cliffs of Dover were sighted and a pilot came aboard our ship to take us through the English Channel into the North Sea. We docked in Bremerhaven on October 21st and boarded trains for the overnight trip to Camp Y-79, a tent city consisting of hundreds of tents that was to be the "staging" area for all units of the 43rd Infantry Division. The MP company was billeted at Camp Y-79 for about 5 days, leaving for Augsburg, Germany, on October 28.

I was among a small contingent of Military Police who remained at Camp Y-79 on special assignment while the remainder of the Division, which was coming overseas in four separate increments, arrived and were processed through Camp Y-79 prior to departing to their final destinations in Southern Germany. Our duties, in addition to policing the Camp Y-79 area, included patroling the City of Mannheim for any military personnel who were found in restricted areas, AWOL, or in violation of curfew restrictions.

This special assignment lasted for approximately 6 weeks, during which time we took up residence in a military hangar in close proximity to Camp Y-79 that was half-full of mattresses, blankets, pillows, etc. This arrangement was great for us, particularly since Camp Y-79 had become a huge mud hole due to excessive rain during this 6 week period. Our special detail ended in November and we joined our fellow MPs who had relocated to Flak Kaserne, in Augsburg, Germany. The 43rd Infantry Division Headquarters was also located at Flak Kaserne.

CHRISTMAS WITH THE RUSSIANS…1951

I spent most of December, 1951, including my first Christmas away from home, on special assignment with 8 to 10 other Military Policemen, in Munsingen, Germany, a small community located in close proximity to the US-Russian Border in Northern Germany. Snow in the area measured upwards of 4 feet throughout our stay.

Our assignment was to patrol the area, including the city of Munsingen, on what I recall was a 24/7 schedule, and to immediately report the presence of any military personnel, US or Foreign, observed in the area. No military personnel were seen in the city, however our patrols included an open area where we could see the border fence about a mile in the distance and the Russian manned watch towers perched atop the fence line.

BACK TO SCHOOL... OBERAMMERGAU, GERMANY

Upon returning to our MP headquarters in Augsburg, I was told to pack my bags as I was scheduled to attend the European Command Military Police School in Oberammergau, Germany, starting January 16 through February 21, 1952.

I was elated. Oberammergau is about 50 miles from Augsburg and 18 miles from Garmisch-Partenkirchen, known as the playground of Europe for military personnel. Garmisch is a very beautiful mountain resort community situated in the Bavarian Alps at the foot of the Zugspitz Mountain, the highest mountain in Germany at 9,000 feet above sea level. The top of the Zugspitz is reachable by cable car, a very exciting 25 minute ride over extremely rugged mountain terrain.

At the base of the Zugspitz is a beautiful lake, The Eibsee, with a 5 star hotel, beach, etc. At that time it was for military personnel only at a nightly cost of $1.00 (yes, one dollar),and you were allowed one guest at no additional cost. WHAT A SETUP!!

The rooms were large, the food was great, ballroom dancing nightly, and everything else to make your stay a memorable one. I spent many a night enjoying all the amenities offered at the hotel during my 3 year assignment in Germany.

I should also mention that the 1952 Winter Olympics were held in Garmisch during my 5 weeks of school and I took every opportunity to attend several of the events including the ski jumping, giant slalom and the individual figure skating.

Back to military police school…there were approximately 20 students in the class, including Navy Shore Patrol, Air Force Police and Army Military Police. I was the only student from the 43rd Infantry Division Military Police Company having had approximately 9 months of MP experience.

I was at an advantage over many of the students who had little or no military police experience. That is not to say that I found the classes boring or didn't benefit from them, I did, particularly in traffic accident investigations, barrack larcenies investigation techniques and tools, riot control, self-defense, ground rules in determining military versus civilian police jurisdiction at a crime scene, etc.

During one of the Sundays I climbed the Kofel Mountain. It wasn't anything like climbing a "real" mountain, but it got progressively more difficult the higher I climbed. It took a total of about 6 hours to ascend and descend the mountain.

The highlight of my weeks of school in Oberammergau was meeting Sylvia Mitterhuber, a waitress in our school cafeteria and the most beautiful young lady in Germany. Our attraction to each other was immediate and our courtship simmered for about 10 months at which time the immigration papers that she and her sister Edith had filed to immigrate to Canada were approved.

We spent virtually every week-end together, spending Saturday afternoons at the Olympic sites, and evenings eating and dancing in the local clubs. Weekend commuting between Oberammergau and Garmisch was available thanks to a free military shuttle bus between the 2 cities. The last bus left Garmisch for Oberammergau at midnight. This was most convenient, especially since I stayed at her parents' house (under the watchful eye of her father) rather than returning to the school barracks.

I completed the Military Police Course on Feb,21, 1952. achieving an academic rating of SUPERIOR. This rating qualified me to return to the school to take the criminal investigator's course which I did in July, 1952.

During the intervening 4 months I was able to spend most weekends with Sylvia. It was about a 2 hour train ride and the schedule was great. I left Augsburg about 1:00 PM Saturday afternoon and Sylvia always met the train, rain or shine, when it arrived in Oberammergau.about 3:00PM.

I should mention that I fell asleep on one of my return train rides back to Augsburg and didn't wake up until I was about 100 miles north of Augsburg. I jumped off the train at the first stop after waking up and learned that the next southbound train that would stop in Augsburg wouldn't be arriving there until about 8:00 AM, arriving in Augsburg at 10:00 AM. I called my First Sargeant to advise him of my situation and expected arrival time in Augsburg. He had no problem and no disciplinary action was taken.

Although there were no Olympics, we would often go into Garmisch and take the cable car to the top of the Zugspitz, which was snow covered all year, to watch the skiers, sightseeing, and patronizing the restaurant that had 360 degree viewing through windows inside the restaurant.

We often attended a Saturday night volksfest (a gala affair of beer drinking, singing and dancing) at the Wittlesbach Hotel in Oberammergau. The accordionist of the group used to let me play his accordion during their intermission breaks. I loved it and so did those enjoying the evening, mostly native residents of Oberammergau.

Sundays began with a barber shave by Sylvia's dad who had a barbershop in his house. It was then to church followed by a German home cooked dinner thanks to her mom. To help with the family finances, I used to bring coffee, sugar, cigarettes, etc. from the Post Exchange and also bought the meat (sauerbraten, wiener schnitzels, or whatever) for the Sunday dinner.

Depending on the weather, and whether Sylvia's mom and dad took an afternoon walk after dinner, our afternoons were spent either in their apartment alone or taking a walk ourselves through some of the beautiful countryside surrounding Oberammergau, often stopping for a beer or two along the way. Did we have a preference as to which option we preferred?…You bet we did!!

BACK TO OBERAMMERGAU... CRIMINAL INVESTIGATION SCHOOL

On July 9, 1951, I returned to Oberammergau to attend the 5 weeks Criminal Investigators' Course. It was great...no more weekly round trips between Augsburg and Oberammergau for at least five weeks.

The criminal investigation classes were extremely interesting and involved various scenarios of mock crime scenes on and off the school premises, including aggravated assaults, a fatal hit and run accident, a rape in a local apartment building, etc. The school staff played roles as suspects and victims in the various scenarios. From the students' perspective, the staff was extremely uncooperative in sharing their knowledge about or involvement in the "mock" crimes under investigations.

Thanks to a bit of private coaching by Sylvia's older sister, a member of the training staff who played major roles in the crime scenarios, I learned that they were instructed to temper their degree of cooperation in the conduct of investigations based upon the demeanor and attitude of the investigator(s) in their treatment of suspects and/or victims during the investigation. Accusations of guilt that were not supported by the evidence, outbursts of anger, cursing, etc. were not tolerated. Fairness with firmness in bringing an investigation to a reasonable conclusion based upon the evidence and facts discovered or developed during the course of the investigation was essential. I graduated from the Criminal Investigators' Course with an Academic Rating of Superior on August 14, 1952.

CRIMINAL INVESTIGATIONS... LIFE CHALLENGES

Upon my return to Augsburg I was relieved of routine military police duties and assigned to the Provost Marshals' office as the military police criminal investigator for the 43rd Infantry Division.

My investigative responsibilities included working with agents of the Augsburg Detachment of the 13th Military Police Criminal Investigation Division, headquartered in Munich, Germany and reporting to the Office of the Provost Marshal General of the U.S. Army.

Investigations involving troops of the 43rd Infantry Division, as well as other military units in the Augsburg area, involved a coordinated effort between the 13th Military Police Criminal Investigation unit and my office, representing the Provost Marshal and Commanding General of the 43rd Infantry Division.

The following are examples of investigations involving 43rd Infantry Division soldiers for which I was primarily responsible. Let me say at the very beginning that any time I interrogated a suspect involving any crime for which he/she might be Court Martialed, I was required to read them Article 31 of the Uniform Code of Military Justice, informing them that they had the right to remain silent and that anything they might say could be used against them in court. I never failed to follow this requirement.

FATAL AUTOMOBILE ACCIDENT

A 43rd Infantry Division soldier drove his car up on the sidewalk in downtown Augsburg one evening killing an 18 year old boy. A sobriety test showed that the driver was intoxicated. At that time the military required an autopsy be performed on the victim of any fatal accident in which the death was allegedly caused by a member of the military services. Hence, an autopsy was required and conducted on the dead 18 year old. It was determined that death was caused from injuries resulting from the accident.

About 2 months later, much to my surprise, the 16 year old brother of the 18 year old who had been killed came to my office for help. His 18 year old brother was still in the city morgue because the family did not have the money to bury him. His mother was widowed and his brother was the only "bread winner" in the family.

I asked and was told that the burial would cost about 400 Deutsche Marks ($100.00). I immediately made arrangements to withdraw $100.00 from my soldier's deposit account and gave it to the boy, with the understanding that if the soldier's company unit decided to take up a collection for the family (most military units did this under such circumstances), and the collection exceeded $100, I would want the $100 returned to me. However, if a collection was not taken, no repayment would be necessary or expected.

I immediately went to the soldier's company commander and told him of the family's plight and that I had given the brother $100 with the understanding that the $100 would be returned to me in the event his company took up a collection and the amount equaled or exceeded $100. He agreed to discuss a collection with the company leaders and would get back with me. The next day I received a call from the Regimental Commander, a full Colonel, saying he wanted to see me right away.

I drove out to his office. He invited me in, closed the door and immediately began chewing me out for obligating his men to make a payment to the family of the 18 year old German who had been killed in the accident. I immediately assured him that I had done nothing of the kind and that his men were under no obligation whatsoever to make any payment to the family or me. He continued to rant and rave about "Who the hell did I think I was," etc. etc. After about 10 minutes he told me to leave…I responded with a salute and left.

I returned to my office, called the company commander involved and asked that he totally disregard everything we had discussed the previous day regarding the fatal automobile accident involving one of his men. He said that would be fine with him, but that he had heard some scuttle-butt to the effect that some of his men wanted to do something for the family. I assured him that that was totally up to him and his men and that I had removed myself totally from any further involvement. Well, about 3 weeks later the 16 year old came back to my office to pay me the 400 Deutsch Marks I had given him. I understand the company collected almost $400 (1600 Deutsch Marks). I was so pleased, more so for the family than having the $100 returned to me.

MURDER AND RAPE

I was called into the Provost Marshal's office early one morning and told that I would be accompanying him to the Hohenfelds maneuver area to investigate the murder of a German doctor and the raping of his wife and their domestic maid by 2 soldiers on maneuvers in the area. We flew to the maneuver area in a military plane and were taken to the command post of the military unit of the soldiers involved.

We learned that the soldiers had been identified and were in custody. My job was to obtain statements from the victims as to what occurred, secure positive identification of the suspects by the victims and interrogate the suspects with regard to their alleged involvement in the murder and rapes.

I learned from the doctor's wife that two soldiers had come to the front door of their home after dark the previous evening complaining of severe headaches. Her husband invited them into the house and went to his office area to obtain medication for their pain. Upon his return, one of the soldiers hit him over the head with a 5 gallon glass container of alcohol. The doctor fell to the floor and both assailants picked him up and threw him out a kitchen window to the ground below.

One of the soldiers then grabbed the doctor's wife, took her into a bedroom and began raping her. The domestic maid, hearing the commotion, came down the stairs from her room and was grabbed by the second soldier who forced her back upstairs and raped her in her bedroom. I understand the doctor's body was found outside the kitchen window.

I interrogated both assailants who admitted to hitting the doctor over the head with the large glass container and the raping of both women. Both soldiers were tried by a General Court Martial and were sentenced to death.

Since this was the first case I had ever investigated that resulted in a death sentence, I was a bit shaken when the sentence was read. However, the soldiers were not…I saw them both under guard in the mess hall that evening and one was joking with the other about getting their necks stretched.

PROSTITUTION RING BUSTED

The Provost Marshal was tipped off that a Major was transporting prostitutes into the Bachelor Officers Quarters (BOQ) in the Flak Kaserne on Saturday evenings. I was given the assignment to investigate the allegation.

Since officers entering the kaserne via the main gate would normally be waived through without any question, or determining the identification of passengers in the car, the possibility of this occurring without detection was quite possible. I obtained the Major's name and the license plate number of his vehicle.

An "alert" was issued that if a car with the designated license plate attempted to enter the kaserne it was to be stopped and the names and addresses of any occupants in the vehicle, including the driver, were to be taken. Because of the Major's rank, the Military Police Duty Officer on duty the following Saturday was also put on notice and was at the MP Desk adjacent to the gate during the evening hours. The suspect's car arrived at the gate the next Saturday evening and the Duty Officer took over and ordered the women into the MP Station where their identification information was recorded in spite of threats of retribution by the Major. After the requested information was obtained the Major turned his car around and left with the 4 women.

During the next couple of weeks I had each of the 4 women come into my office where I took a brief statement in which they admitted to having been approached by the Major and had entered the Bachelor Officers Quarters for the purpose of having sex for money that was arranged by the Major. Each prostitute was in possession of a valid prostitution license issued by the Augsburg City Health Department.

Since the major denied having met the women, or transporting them to the Bachelor Officers Quarters in Flak Kaserne, I took the next step. I arranged to have a line-up to include the suspect Major and 5 other officers and ask each prostitute to identify which officer among the six had contacted and transported them to the Bachelor's Officer Quarters for purposes of having sex for money. The line-up was scheduled for 1:00 PM on a specified date at the Bachelor Officer Quarters.

I was about to leave my office at 12:45 PM on the specified day to conduct the line-up when I received a call that the Major had just shot himself in the head with a 45 Caliber pistol and was enroute by ambulance to the 11th Army Field Hospital located less than a half mile from where the line-up was scheduled to take place.

I immediately went to the hospital expecting to be told he was dead and when the death certificate would be available for me to pick up. Much to my surprise, he had been admitted to the hospital. The angle of the pistol at the time he fired it caused the bullet to ricochet off his skull and exit on the opposite side of his head without penetrating the skull or entering his brain. About a month later he was transferred to a military post in France.

GRAND LARCENCY

The Provost Marshal came into my office one morning with a letter addressed to the Commanding General of the 43rd Infantry Division from the parents of a soldier who had committed suicide. The letter was in reference to their son's personal property that had been returned to them. Specifically, their letter stated that their son had 2 rings and a wristwatch which were not included in the inventory of their son's personal belongings.

I made an appointment with the dead soldier's company commander and learned the identity of the officer responsible for gathering and returning the soldier's belongings to his next of kin. I requested and received a copy of the documentation, including the inventory of items returned, that was prepared and signed by the Major responsible for returning the items to the family. The rings and watch were not included in the list of inventoried items returned.

I called the Major and requested an appointment to meet with him. He asked why and I told him it was in regard to a letter addressed to General Gailey, (Commanding General of the 43rd Infantry Division at the time) regarding items missing from the inventory of personal belongings returned to the next of kin for which he was responsible. He denied any knowledge of what I was talking about.

I went to his office at an agreed upon time dressed in civilian clothes which was permissible as an accredited agent of the Provost Marshal's office. He immediately ordered me to tell him my military rank, which I refused to do, but did show him my credentials issued by the Provost Marshal General. This was unsatisfactory and he refused to discuss the matter any further until I disclosed my rank.

I should note that one of the points stressed during the criminal investigation course in Oberammergau was to dress in civilian clothes when conducting investigations of individuals who outranked you, particularly in those situations when you were an enlisted man dealing with an officer.

I then called Major Nathan, the Provost Marshal for the Augsburg Military District and advised him of my problem. Major Nathan had me put the Major on the phone and he, Major Nathan, ordered him to get into my car and come to his office immediately. He then challenged Major Nathan's order, demanding that Major Nathan tell him his date of rank, thus questioning Major Nathan's authority to give him a direct order. This was the wrong thing to do…I heard Major Nathan holler into the phone something to the effect that if he was not in his office in 15 minutes he would order a team of Military Policeman to arrest him and bring him to his office.

The Major reluctantly got into my car and accompanied me to Major Nathan's office where he was arrested by Major Nathan himself for suspicion of grand larceny and perhaps other charges as well. I am not certain what the final disposition was in this case, but understand the Major returned the stolen property and was transferred out of the 43rd Infantry Division to another military unit in Germany.

SYLVIA LEAVES FOR CANADA

In the summer of 1952, Sylvia and her sister Edith immigrated to Canada. Both had sponsors, and each would be employed by their respective sponsor as a domestic. I gave her money to take with her so that she would be able to purchase any necessities she might need until she started being paid. Regrettably, she and her sister would be living about 50 miles apart. Needless to say, our last weekend together was an absolute nightmare in the "heartache" department.

I didn't get a letter from her for about a month and when I did, I could hardly believe it. She was taking care of 3 or 4 kids, cooking for the family, doing their laundry and keeping the house picked-up and clean, plus anything else they wanted her to do. Her day started early and didn't end until the kids were in bed. She was sssooo home sick. She was under a 1 or 2 year obligation to remain with her sponsor. Hence, returning to Germany, as I suggested, was not an option. I wrote often in an attempt to help keep her spirits up, but her letters became less frequent with the passing of time.

I began a casual relationship with Lieselotte (Lilo) Kaufman, whom I married in November 1954. Lilo was the sister of my tailor, Josef Kaufmann, a Master Tailor. Josef was an English speaking, ex American POW, who had the reputation of making "American" style suits. He was the tailor for most of the agents in the 13th Military Police Criminal Investigation Detachment (MP-CID) in Augsburg. He and I hit it off from the very beginning. I remember that one of my first dates with Lilo was joining Josef and his fiancée, Hildegard, on a one day trip by train to Munich to attend the Octoberfest. It was a real fun day and the first of many "double" dating events.

UNIVERSITY OF VIENNA... HERE I COME

During the summer of 1953 I learned that a 2 week course in "Psychology of Criminal Interrogation" and "Scientific Criminal Investigation" was being offered in English by the Institute of Criminology at the University of Vienna, Vienna, Austria, by Dr. Roland Grassberger, Director of the Institute. Sargeant R.B. Stanton, acting Director of the 13th Military Police Criminal Investigation Office in Augsburg at the time, was one of about 10 Military Police criminal investigation agents selected to attend the two week course.

Recognizing the potential benefits that I might gain by attending the course, particularly if I decided to make a career in the military as a criminal investigator, I obtained the details from Stanton regarding the timing, cost, etc. to attend the course. I then approached my immediate supervisor, Lt Colonel Muncie, 43rd Division Provost Marshal and asked if he would allow me to take personal leave time to attend the course provided I paid my own expenses including tuition, travel, lodging, etc for the 2 week period. He not only approved it, he applauded my interest and willingness to improve my interrogation and investigation skills at my own expense.

The course was scheduled to begin on Monday, Sept 7, 1953 and end on Friday, September 18, 1953. I obtained a copy of the registration form from Stanton and called Dr. Grassberger's office to ascertain if he would allow me to attend. His answer was "yes," provided I paid the tuition fee. I don't recall how much the fee was, but I completed the registration form, obtained an international money order to cover the tuition and sent it to him. Within a week or so I received a confirmation letter approving my attendance.

I was able to make reservations for a room at the Regina Hotel in Vienna, the hotel recommended by the school, as it was only a block or two from the Institute where classes were to be held. The class schedule that accompanied my confirmation letter identified classroom hours from 8:00AM to noon (Psychology of Criminal Interrogation) and 1:00 PM to 5:00 PM (Scientific Criminal Investigation). It also noted that daily homework would average 4 hours per day. A pretty tough schedule, but I was ready!

The only train that US military personnel were allowed to travel on between Munich, Germany and Vienna, Austria at that time was the Oriental Express. This restriction was imposed because most of the trip was through the USSR occupied sector of Germany. Also, we were required to travel in uniform and were subject to being searched, including our luggage, by USSR military personnel upon entering and leaving the USSR occupation zone of Germany.

I immediately purchased my ticket to depart Munich, Germany for Vienna, Austria, Friday morning, the 4th of September, rather than take a chance that the tickets might be sold out, or that I might be "bumped" or put on standby, if I waited until the weekend. Also, I was looking forward to having a couple of extra days to become acquainted with Vienna before classes started.

The 4th of September finally arrived and I went to Munich

(about 50 miles from Augsburg) and caught the Oriental Express to Vienna. The train was packed with mostly civilians. Each car had several compartments, each compartment capable of seating 8 people. The aisle connecting the compartments was along the inside of the car where passengers entered and exited the train. I found a corner adjacent to one of these stairwells and used my suitcase for a seat.

After traveling about 30 minutes, an attractive young lady approached me and invited me to follow her as there was a seat available in her compartment. I grabbed my suitcase and followed her to her compartment with an empty seat next to hers. During our conversation enroute to Vienna, I learned that her name was Joyce (what a coincidence) and that she was a TWA airlines stewardess on her way to spend the weekend in Vienna before boarding a flight to London and back to New York.

Our conversation was suddenly interrupted when 2 Russian soldiers barged into our compartment demanding everyone stand up and open our suitcases on our seats. They were extremely rude, dumping everything out of Joyce's purse and our suitcases onto our seats in two big piles. We were the only Americans in that compartment, and the only ones who had their luggage dumped on their seats.

We had a most enjoyable trip together. By the time we reached Vienna we were in complete agreement that we would spend the weekend touring Vienna together, especially since neither of us had ever been there.

Upon arriving at the Vienna train station we took a taxi to the Regina Hotel and dropped off our luggage. We asked our cab driver if he could recommend a special restaurant for us as this was our first visit to Vienna. Without any hesitation he recommended the Scharlachberg restaurant/nightclub that was perched atop a small mountain overlooking the city of Vienna. It was beautiful!!

We sipped on some delicious domestic white wine from Grensing, a suburb of Vienna. We made our dinner selections, which were superb, and since we were obviously Americans, the attention and services we received were also superb. We danced away the evening to the most beautiful Viennese music while observing the lights and beauty of the City of Vienna below. Neither of us could believe that what started off to be a day of travel alone to a city we had never visited before, could have turned out to be so beautiful. Our evening ended and we returned to the hotel, reminiscing over our experiences of the day and looking forward to what the next day would bring.

Our Saturday began with a walk along a sidewalk that was adjacent to a well marked boundary identifying it as the USSR sector of Vienna and OFF LIMITS to Americans. The most prominent landmark was the Prada Ferris Wheel, located in an amusement park about 2 blocks inside the Russian Sector, which at that time was the largest ferris wheel in the world.

Along the way we stopped for breakfast at a sidewalk café that was also advertising tours of the city. We selected a 4-hour bus tour of the cultural highlights of Vienna, including a drive through Grenzing and the **Schönbrunn Palace.**

We thoroughly enjoyed our tour through Grenzing, especially the sidewalk cafes, music playing in the streets, restaurants with outside patios, etc. We liked it so well we decided to go back there for dinner. It was about a 20 minute drive by taxi and once there we strolled through the streets until we found a restaurant with a beautiful patio decorated with colored outdoor lights and a small orchestra playing Viennese music. It was the perfect setting for a beautiful evening. I don't remember what we ate, but it was delicious!! We reveled in the moment, enjoyed a marvelous evening together and retired to our hotel sometime after mid-night.

Our time together on Sunday was pretty short as Joyce had to catch a flight out of Vienna for London shortly after noon. We enjoyed another brunch together and reminisced over what an unexpectedly marvelous weekend we had shared together.

Following our brunch, we returned to the hotel, got Joyce's luggage and I accompanied her to the airport where we hugged for several minutes. When it came time to part, we said our good byes and waved for the last time as she entered the airport terminal. I missed her terribly as I returned to my hotel. Stanton arrived later that afternoon and we went out for a few drinks and dinner that evening.

Our classes began promptly at 8:00 AM, Monday morning, September 7, 1953, with 10 in the class; 8 U.S. military police investigators, 1 agent from Scotland Yard and 1 female investigator from Israel. Dr. Grassberger passed out a pile of reading material to be read during the 2 week course, the substance of which would be included in the final exam. He also addressed class attendance, advising that for the benefit of the whole class, only one late absence of less than 10 minutes would be permitted. A second absence or a first absence of more than 10 minutes would result in immediate dismissal from the course. During the first week the lady from Israel came to class about 2 hours late and was immediately dismissed from the class.

Classes were divided between a classroom and Dr. Grassberger's Crime Museum. On occasion he would lecture in the classroom and then take us into the museum to illustrate or discuss a specific point. I recall several skulls he had that showed the amount of trauma or destruction resulting from a specific weapon or firearm, the effect of the trajectory of the projectile, distance of the weapon from the victim when fired, etc. He also had several samples of the damage/disfiguration of body parts (face, skin hands, etc) as a way of identifying the weapon used and its proximity to the victim when fired.

His lectures on the psychology of interrogation were most

interesting with respect to emphasizing the suffering he/she has caused his/her victim and family and the suspects' physical reactions...sweaty hands, avoiding looking directly at you during interrogation, continuous licking of his/her lips, etc. Dr.Grassberger also addressed the "good guy"-"bad guy" scenario and when to employ this interrogation technique. Other details of interrogation techniques were addressed during the two week program.

The 2 weeks passed very quickly. Stanton, a Captain from Bremerhaven and I signed up for a tour of Grenzing Saturday evening. It consisted of a tour of 4 wine cellars where we each received a viertel of wine (a 6 ounce glass of wine) in the wine cellar and another viertel in the restaurant/guest room or patio. The tour also included a dinner at one of the 4 restaurants of our choosing. We selected one with a large outside patio, attractive lady guests, and dancing to a great 4 or 5 piece orchestra. We left the tour at this point and spent a delightful, fun-filled evening of dining and dancing, returning to our hotel sometime before morning.

Our second week of classes was just as exciting as the first week...more of the same, but in greater detail. The presentation of our certificates of having successfully completed the course were presented on Friday afternoon, September 18th, 1953.

During the presentation, Dr Grassberger congratulated each of us for our active participation in one of the finest classes he had ever taught.

Stanton and I returned to Augsburg on Saturday, September 20th via the Oriental Express. Again, Russian soldiers boarded the train when we entered the Russian occupied zone of Germany, but no searches of suitcases were made. Stanton was Chief of the 13th Military Police Criminal Investigation unit in Augsburg at the time and although I was not yet a CID agent, we had a lot in common to share on our "Ride Home."

DECISION TIME…AGAIN

Upon my return to the office, I was advised that my 3 year enlistment in the U.S. Army was approaching the "90 day window" for rotation back to the States and discharge. Although Lilo and I had been dating a relatively short time, we were very much in love and had decided that we would get married so that she could accompany me back to the States versus my returning to the States and then returning to Germany as a civilian to get married. This option would have been much more expensive, hence we decided we would pursue getting married before I left.

Little did I know what was involved in getting married. First, I had to get permission from the Army. This involved completing a horrendous number of multi-page forms. Also, they would have to do a background investigation to determine if there was any reason why they should not grant Lilo a Visa to enter the U.S.

Bottom line…getting married before my rotation date was impossible. I also wanted to gain additional experience as an accredited criminal investigator in the 13th Military Police Criminal Investigation Detachment in Augsburg, and thus be an agent under the jurisdiction of the Provost Marshal General of the U.S. Army. I was certain that this additional experience would substantially enhance my opportunity for advancement if I decided to make a career in the military, and also, my opportunity to become an FBI agent in the event I should leave the Army and seek employment with the Federal Bureau of Investigation.

My plan for accomplishing both objectives, getting married and also being transferred to the 13th MP CID, was to extend my enlistment one year, from 3 years to 4 years, contingent upon my being transferred from the 43rd Infantry Division to the 13th MP CID in Augsburg. With the help of Lt Col. Muncie, my immediate supervisor and Provost Marshal of the 43rd Division, my proposal was accepted. My transfer to the 13th MP CID was effective on or about December 1, 1953, and my enlistment in the Army was extended from January 14, 1954 to January 14, 1955.

I would be remiss if I did not include a brief statement noting that my mom was very opposed to my extending my enlistment and begged me to please come home. I understood her rationale completely and I would be telling my son or daughter the same thing under similar circumstances. I attempted to persuade her that one more year of criminal investigation experience could pay big dividends in pursuing a career that I found very exciting and challenging. My decision to stay hurt her terribly, but I believe she understood my reasons for doing what I did??

results. In anticipation that this would become an issue, the technician who conducted the analysis of the molds at the crime lab in Frankfurt came to Augsburg from Frankfurt and was called to take the witness stand. His testimony was to the effect that the molds had been taken by an individual well trained in the procedure and were among the best he had ever analyzed.

I was also grilled by the defense lawyers as to when the molds were taken, before or after midnight, on the day Thomas was arrested. I had consistently testified that it was before midnight. However, the defense asked that the record of the Court Martial be searched, alleging that at one point in my testimony during the previous day or two, I had testified that it was possible that it might have been after midnight. In making this challenge, they alleged that I had perjured myself and my testimony should be disregarded. The purpose of the challenge was to discredit my testimony, since the timing of when the molds were taken was immaterial to the analysis results.

It was at this point that I heard Thomas ask his lawyers why they were trying to "mess me up" when he was the one who had killed the 4 people. I believe the defense had pretty well exhausted their defense arguments for an acquittal and were prepared to accept a guilty finding by the members of the General Court Martial.

Notwithstanding the fact that my investigation and testimony at his Court Martial was the evidence upon which he was convicted, Thomas considered me his friend, perhaps his only friend. I returned to Germany on vacation during the summer of 1957 and was told by my former secretary who was still employed at the Augsburg MP-CID office at that time, that the office had received notification that Thomas had been executed at Fort Leavenworth, Kansas.

WITNESSES NAME SLAYER OF SARGEANT

The investigation in this case was pretty well limited to the positive identification of those involved, determining the cause of death and obtaining statements from the principle witnesses as to what they observed throughout the ordeal.

My specific involvement in this case was again, flying by military aircraft to the Military Police Crime Laboratory in Frankfurt to witness the autopsy of Sargeant T. J. Ramsey and to recover the bullet(s) as they were discovered by the coroner performing the autopsy.

It was determined that one bullet caused the death of Sargeant Ramsey, which the coroner tracked from the time it entered his neck, passed through his heart, a lung, plus a few other body organs. I observed the path of the bullet as it was revealed by the coroner to its final location which was just under the skin in one of Ramsey's buttocks. The coroner had me remove the bullet with a pair of forceps. I then marked the flat surface of the projectile with the letter "'K" to assure the integrity of the chain of custody. I returned to Augsburg with the bullet in my possession until it was logged into the vault where all evidence was held pending its use during a Court Martial or other approved disposition.

Upon my return to Augsburg, ballistic examination of the bullet I had recovered from Ramseys' body revealed that it had been fired from the same weapon recovered at the crime scene, thus establishing the fact that the bullet that killed Ramsey was fired from the weapon used by Smith.

While the cases cited above stand-out among those I investigated during my year with the 13th MP-CID, I worked a number of other cases including the rape of an 84 year old woman working in a field on her farm, aggravated assaults, personal robbery of a taxi driver who received a fractured skull when struck on the head with the butt of a Colt 44 revolver, suicides, and a race riot between blacks and Hispanics resulting in 2 deaths.

WEDDING BELLS ARE RINGING, NOVEMBER 23RD, 1954

I spent many hours completing pages of military forms required for marriage to a Foreign National, plus lectures by commanders and Chaplains to discourage marriage to a Foreign National and discouraging the "bride to be" to marry an American because of the thousands of miles and years of separation from family that she will have to endure for the rest of her life. Notwithstanding, we were successful in arranging our wedding within the required 30 days from the date of our scheduled departure from Bremerhaven for rotation back to the States, which was scheduled for December 15, 1954.

The photo attests to the fact that our wedding was a very happy and joyous occasion.

OUR TRIP BACK TO THE STATES

We arrived in Bremerhaven for our "cruise" back to the States, departing on December 15, 1954, scheduled to arrive in New York on December 27th. The rumor aboard ship was that we would arrive in New York on Christmas Day. Well, we were within 6 hours of the New York docks on the 25th, but because of lack of docking space our ship would not be docking until the 27th.

Lilo was seasick from the time she boarded ship until she went ashore in New York. We were only allowed to be together on deck…we couldn't even eat together or sleep in the same room. This made it particularly difficult. We had decided on one lounge area on the main deck where we would meet every morning about 8:00 AM. Because of being seasick, Lilo would stay in bed as long as she could, so I spent many hours waiting in the lounge alone.

I understood perfectly, and even when we were in the lounge together it was not pleasant as sick as she was. Anyway, we finally docked early on the morning of the 27th at the Brooklyn Navy Yard. After pushing our way to look over the side of the ship, we spotted my mom and dad standing on the dock along with a few hundred others. After about a half hour we were able to get their attention.

We got off the boat about an hour later and were able to meet up with them on the dock. Since Lilo and I had to take a bus to the hotel for processing, we were not able to go with them. We gave them the name and address of the hotel and met them there. We spent about 2 hours together…it was so great after such a long separation. They left to go back to Connecticut and Lilo and I went to briefings the next 3 days. Bottom line was that I was NOT going to re-enlist. I PASSED my physical and was Honorably Discharged about noon on December 30, 1954.

We left for Hartford, Connecticut on the next scheduled train out of Grand Central Station, arriving in Hartford late in the afternoon. My mom and dad met us in Hartford and drove us to their house where we stayed for about 3 weeks. What a reception with family and friends when we arrived, and WOW, WHAT A NEW YEAR'S CELEBRATION WE HAD THAT YEAR!!!

In closing this phase of my life, I must emphasize that my 4 years in the military were extremely challenging and exciting. I am so appreciative and grateful for the support of my parents and family and the hundreds of military friends and associates who guided and assisted me in achieving a level of maturity and recognition beyond my every expectation. As the saying goes, "I entered the service as a boy and came out a man."

PERIOD OF MILITARY SERVICE

January 15, 1951–December 30, 1954

I CLOSE THIS PART OF MY LIFE'S STORY WITH A SALUTE TO

EVERYONE WHO HAS OR IS CURRENTLY SERVING IN THE MILITARY SERVICES.

WHAT NEXT— COLLEGE VERSUS EMPLOYMENT

Following a quick "get reacquainted" visit with aunts, uncles, friends, etc. in the Storrs area, I contacted Congressman Tony Sadlak, Congressman-at-Large for the State of Connecticut at the time. After giving him a quick summary of my criminal investigation experience in the military, I asked for his assistance in arranging for me to meet with appropriate Federal Bureau of Investigation staff in Washington, D.C. to explore employment possibilities with the FBI. Within a day or two he called me back with the name and phone number of a member of the FBI Human Resources organization who was willing to meet with me. I called the individual and set up an appointment to meet with him in D.C. a few days later.

In preparation for my meeting I completed a Federal employment application, gathered appropriate military records to take with me, and got train tickets for my wife and me to go to Washington, D.C. What an exciting and memorable ride that was…the same train I had taken so many times 4 years earlier while stationed at Camp Pickett!

The individual I met with was most complimentary of my achievements as a criminal investigator in the military. However, he was quick to point out that without a college degree my career with the FBI would be limited to that of a laboratory technician, finger printing analyst, etc. He urged me to get a college degree and then get back in contact with the Bureau if I was still interested in employment with them. I thanked him for his time and accepted his advice to pursue a college degree.

FINALLY A COLLEGE STUDENT

Upon my return to Storrs, I immediately contacted the admissions office to schedule an appointment to take the entrance exam one more time. I took it and passed it this time. However, Tom Roberts, the admissions officer when I had taken and failed the entrance exam prior to enlisting in the Army in 1951, advised me that although I had passed the exam I really wasn't "college caliber material." That was all I needed to hear...it provided me all the incentive I needed to get a Bachelor of Science Degree in three and a half years, plus one summer school session and a Master's Degree in Public Administration 2 years later.

I had about 2 weeks to register and prepare my course schedule before the spring semester began. In addition, I also had to buy a car and find a place to live.

I purchased a used car from a dealer where my dad bought his cars, a Dodge convertible. It served us well.

My dad had also been checking around for a place for us to live...obviously he and my mom wanted to make sure we weren't planning on living with them while I went through college. He located a 21 foot house trailer for sale in a trailer park owned and operated by a long time friend of the family. The park was within a mile of the campus.

Unfortunately the trailer did not have a toilet…this meant we would have to use the toilets and showers in a utility building that was a LONG 30 or 40 feet from the entrance to our trailer. The trailer was small, but nice inside, and had a small addition that housed the cooking stove and refrigerator. Most important, it was only $500.00 and the monthly ground rent was only $36.00. We bought it thinking we would only be in it 3 and a half years, but we actually ended up living in it until I got my Master's Degree 5 and a half years later.

We were 1 of 7 couples living in what was an isolated part of the park. It was a congenial group of neighbors, all striving to get through college on limited funds. I was one of three veterans and am still in frequent contact with one of the couples who has since retired to Florida, Jim and Marie Nation.

Returning to the classroom was difficult after being out of school for 5 years. I did get some tutoring from my high school math teacher and also my college English teacher. After the first semester I was able to get along without outside help and my "study discipline" improved with time.

During the school year I worked part-time in the Nutmeg Fountain where I had worked during my high school years. During the summers I worked full-time for the University Farm Department doing a variety of jobs, including hoeing corn, working in hay fields, leveling silage as it was being blown into the several silos adjacent to animal barns around campus, etc. It was hard work, but the pay was good for a summer job.

My wife also worked at the Electro-Motive Manufacturing Company in Willimantic, assembling radio condensers for space communication systems. She worked from 7:00AM until 4:00 PM. We would have to leave our trailer by 6:30 in the morning. A family friend who also worked there used to drop her off at the trailer on her way home. Her job was very monotonous, but paid well. Also, she would be laid off 3 or 4 times during the year for periods of up to six weeks or so.

During my sophomore year I was elected Commander of the local Veterans of Foreign Wars Post. I really enjoyed the comradery, the recognition and appreciation we received through our participation in various memorial services, assisting veteran families when requested, etc.

BACK TO GERMANY FOR A VISIT

Lilo's father died suddenly in the spring of 1957. We made a trip back to Germany that summer to be with her mom and brother. We enjoyed seeing everyone again, family as well as some of the German staff who were still working at the 13th MP-CID office in Augsburg where I had worked prior to returning to the States in 1954.

During our vacation I had the opportunity to manage a large nightclub that was patronized almost exclusively by military personnel. I knew the owner well from my military days in Augsburg. When he learned that I was back on vacation he asked if I would manage his club, "The Atlantic Bar," so that he could go to New York on a month's vacation. I was delighted and so was he. His wife stayed in Augsburg and did all the ordering, bookkeeping, etc. while he was gone. All I had to do was open the club at 6:00PM daily except Sunday, close it at 2:00 AM, and oversee the services and maintain order in the club from 6:00 PM to 2:00 AM.

The Atlantic Bar was a very exclusive club with an intercom system of telephones on every table. There was a number on a small pole next to the phone. If you wanted to contact someone at table number 91 (there were a total of 110 tables and booths with phones) all you had to do was pick up the phone on your table and dial 91.

We also had 2 floor shows nightly, one at 11:00 PM and a second one at 1:00 AM. Each show was different and lasted about 30-45 minutes. I introduced both shows in German and English.

My biggest job was keeping everyone in line and I had plenty of help. We had a bouncer, plus there was a military police jeep with both military and German police parked at the rear of the club most of the time.

GRADUATION MEANT JOB HUNTING

We returned from Germany in mid-August and school started again in September.

I graduated with a BS Degree in June 1958, having taken two courses during one summer session and carrying 21 credits my last semester, including a 1 credit course in floral arrangement that met 2 hours once a week to come up with the magic number of 124 credits for graduation.

My wife persuaded me to take floral arrangement versus soda fountain management which was also a 1 credit course. The reason was that she had learned from one of our neighbors that students in the floral arrangement course were allowed to take their arrangements home after class! It paid off big time...I got an "A" in the class and an "A+" from my wife!

Upon receiving my Bachelor's Degree in June1958, I completed the Federal Employment Application Form and submitted it to the U.S. Civil Service Commission for consideration in filling federal vacancies government wide. I received 2 inquiries of interest, one from the Immigration and Naturalization Service for a position as a border guard along the U.S.-Mexican border and the other was with the Internal Revenue Service, auditing individual income tax returns. I could hardly do my own taxes say nothing about finding errors in the returns filed by others. I declined the opportunity for an interview for both positions.

I also submitted an application to the U.S. Atomic Energy Commission (an independent agency not subject to the formalities of the Civil Service Commission) and was advised by Mattie Pinett, coordinator of their Management Intern Program, that a Master's Degree in Public or Business Administration was required for an internship. She also advised that they select only 10 management interns annually and that advancement opportunities for those selected in prior years had proven to be extremely good. This was an opportunity I could not pass up.

I decided to work full time for a year and start graduate school in September, 1959. I went to work for Milton (Mick) Beebe, a family friend and local construction contractor, primarily road repair, building new sidewalks and paving driveways. One of the first jobs I had was working on replacing wooden planks with concrete planks on a footbridge that spanned the Willimantic River in Willimantic. The footbridge was approximately 2500 feet long and 92 feet above the river.

Our day started with removing up to 100 feet of the wooden planks, chipping the paint off the 2 inch I-beams supporting the planks, repainting the I-beams and replacing the wooden planks with concrete planks that weighed close to 200 pounds each. We walked the 2 inch I-beams and straddled them while chipping and repainting them. As it turned out, only 2 of us, plus Mick, were able to perform the work required at that height above the river. We replaced about 100 feet of planks per day, hence it took us about a month to complete the job.

ME...IN GRADUATE SCHOOL????

In August I applied for admission to Graduate School and was accepted for the program leading to a Master's Degree in Public Administration. There were 4 of us in this program and Dr. Karl Bosworth was our Graduate School Counselor. One of the four was the Mayor of the City of Manchester, Connecticut, a relatively large metropolitan area just East of Hartford and 20 miles from campus. The remaining 3 of us lived in the Storrs area.

Requirements for the program included satisfactory completion of eight, 3 credit graduate level courses/studies, including a Master's Thesis, plus a 2 hour oral exam at the conclusion of the course work. Faculty participation at the oral exam were those Professors who had oversight responsibility over the courses or independent studies completed by the student.

My thesis assignment was in Administrative Law and Dr. Fred Kort, one of the most respected professors on campus, was my oversight professor. Allow me to explain...There are a number of conditions that must be met prior to the implementation of an order generated pursuant to an Administrative Order. These conditions include the timeliness in announcing public hearings regarding the order, the adequacy of the notice in properly advising the public of the subject matter covered by the pending order, etc. At the time of my study I believe there were some 18 conditions that had to be met.

My thesis assignment was to review the Administrative Procedures Act of Ohio as enacted (I believe it was enacted in the late 1930s), and identify the extent to which precedents established in the administration of the Act since its enactment may have changed or impacted these prescribed conditions in the creation or implementation of administrative orders. I spent many, many hours at the University Law School library in Hartford, (30 miles one-way) doing the required research to prepare my thesis.

About half way through the year I found myself wandering off course and unable to follow the plan to achieve the objectives of the study. At that point I tore up my notes and the pages I had typed and started over. I completed the paper and delivered it to Dr. Kort's residence the evening of the day it was due. The text of the study was 97 pages and I received the grade of "K" which stood for "HONORS QUALITY"!!

My oral exam was scheduled on a Saturday morning early in May and 6 of my 7 oversight professors, including Dr. Bosworth, were present. It started off with Dr. Bosworth giving a general summary of my course work and expressing his appreciation to each of the professors for their assistance and oversight in preparing a very complete and meaningful Master's Degree program for me.

The first professor to ask me a question was Dr Linnevold, who had given me an assignment on the implementation/ administration of the Natural Gas Act. I did not understand the question and asked if he would re-state it. He responded to the effect that "understanding the question is part of the exam." At that point, Dr. Bosworth intervened on my behalf indicating that he too did not understand the question and would he please repeat it. At that point Dr. Linnevold got up, left the room and never returned. I should mention that he was the only professor to give me a "C" as a grade on the final report I prepared for him.

The remaining professors each asked me a series of questions on the work I had done and each was very complimentary. The exam lasted the full 2 hours, at which time Dr. Bosworth asked me to leave the room while they evaluated my responses to the questions asked during the exam and whether, in their view, I had met the standards expected of a Master's Degree candidate. I was called back into the room about 15 minutes later and greeted by Dr. Bosworth who shook my hand and congratulated me for having completed the requirements for a Master's Degree in Public Administration. The other professors who participated in the exam also shook my hand and congratulated me.

GRADUATION AND A JOB... HOW SWEET IT IS

At the request of Mattie Pinett, I had submitted an employment application at the end of the first semester, indicating subjects and grades, and my schedule of courses for the second semester. I called her early Monday morning following my orals to let her know I would be receiving my Master's Degree in Public Administration in June.

It was about 3:00 PM on May 19, 1960 (I will never forget it) when my mom drove up to our trailer to say that Mattie Pinett had called the house (we couldn't afford a phone in the trailer) and wanted me to call her back at my earliest opportunity. We went right back to my folks' house and I called her. The essence of her message was," I am pleased to advise you that you have been selected as one of our 1960 management interns." WOW! I had achieved the most important goal in my life!

I reported to the AEC Headquarters building in Germantown, Maryland on June 1 for 4 weeks of general orientation. When the orientation came to a close 4 weeks later, Lilo and I, and our cat Mitzi, headed west to Albuquerque, New Mexico, for 4 months of orientation on the AEC's nuclear weapons program.

We rented a one bedroom apartment in a small development

of perhaps 20 apartments. We had some great neighbors and really enjoyed socializing together at the end of each day. Our next door neighbor was a self-proclaimed master martini maker. I did not care for martinis, but he was also a master at making a great gin and tonic.

We returned to AEC Headquarters early in November for further orientations on the AEC and the long term objectives of the intern program. We were advised that it was the goal of the intern program that each intern spend up to 2 years in an operations office to gain experience from the ground up.

NEW YORK CITY...HERE I COME!!!

Although my preference was to remain at the AEC Headquarters in Germantown, the New York Operations Office had requested that I be transferred to New York to work with the Industrial Relations Director who would be leaving soon. I had met the Director, Hank O'Neil, at the time of the group interview I had with the principal managers of the New York Operations office about mid-way through my spring semester. About two weeks after my interview in New York, I participated in another group interview with Technical and Administrative staff, including Mattie Pinett, at the Atomic Energy Commission Offices in Germantown, Maryland.

I will never forget one of the questions I was asked during my group interview in New York. It went something like this...if you were the Mayor of New York City and had a $10 million surplus in your budget at the end of a fiscal year, would you extend the runways at LaGuardia Airport or hire more police to patrol the streets of New York City. Either answer was correct...they wanted to hear the logic in support of the decision I had selected.

My decision was to extend the runways at LaGuardia to enhance air safety and accommodate additional air traffic, passenger as well as freight, which was currently operating at maximum capacity. Flights in and out of LaGuardia were experiencing major delays, especially during periods of inclement weather, substantially disrupting passenger traffic and jeopardizing air safety in the vicinity of LaGuadia Airport.

As I recall, the mid-air plane crash involving a TWA and, I believe, a United Airlines passenger flight over Long Island occurred a relatively short time prior to my interview. I concluded my remarks with the thought that unless something was done soon to improve safety and accessibility to LaGuardia that those currently struggling to use the airport might seek out other airports in the New York area for flight services.

From the immediate feedback I received from those in the room, my decision and rationale for it had gained the support of those participating in my interview.

We moved to New York in January and lived with college friends in White Plains, New York for 2 or 3 weeks while we looked for an apartment. We located an apartment in the Park City Estates, a new apartment complex of 3 high-rise buildings on the corner of 97th Street and Queens Boulevard on Long Island. We were the first tenants to rent the one-bedroom apartment we selected.

The first time we went into the apartment we were shocked when we saw cock roaches running in all directions. We were told that all buildings in New York City had cock roaches and were advised to stuff all wall and floor openings into the apartment (water pipes, phone lines, etc.) with cotton and putty. I did this and we then sprayed the whole apartment. We continued to see a roach occasionally, but far fewer than when we first walked in.

Our apartment was on the 14th floor of a 24 story building. We had a nice balcony that faced the west and there was also a beautiful colored water fountain in the front of the building. We soon learned that you put glass coasters on top of glasses, not under them, when sitting on the balcony.

My office was located near the Bowery on West Houston Street in lower Manhattan and I would encounter between 2 and 10 residents of the Bowery daily.

The subway was by far the best mode of transportation between our apartment complex and my office. I had about a 3 block walk to the local subway station where I boarded the train. I got off 4 stops later where I caught the red line express that took me to a stop about 4 blocks from my office. It took approximately an hour to get to my office from our apartment. To drive it took about 90 minutes during the rush hour traffic and the daily parking fee I believe was $12.00.

My responsibilities as the Industrial Relations representative for the New York Operations Office was to monitor, approve or send to our Headquarters for approval, the personal services costs that were reimbursable under our contracts with several large industrial firms and universities. Each contract had an Appendix "A" that identified employee salary schedules, benefits, travel costs, etc. that were reimbursable under our contract with them. I had authority to approve most costs with the exception of salaries, bonuses, travel costs, etc. for corporate executives. Their schedule ranges for such costs had to be approved at our Headquarters in Germantown, Maryland. I was then responsible for monitoring their costs for compliance with the schedules approved in Headquarters.

On those occasions when an existing contract was being renewed, or a new contract was being negotiated, I often accompanied the responsible contract administrator to review, negotiate and approve acceptable personal services costs under the contract.

Since my responsibilities covered industrial relations in the broadest sense, I elected to take a 2-semester, 6 credit course on Public Control of Labor Relations at New York University during the 1961 spring and fall semesters. The course covered a detailed analysis of the provisions and applicability of the Taft-Hartley and Davis-Bacon Acts to specific labor situations. It was an interesting course, but I never got involved in any contractor dispute that involved either of these Acts.

A STAR IS BORN!!

One of the highlights of my 2 years in New York was being selected to be on the "Password" television program. The selection process started one night when Lilo and I got tickets to attend the "live" show. When we entered we were given a card to fill out that included name, employer, state of residence, etc. These cards were then collected just prior to the start of the show.

When the show was over, one of the program people came into the audience area and announced that he was going to read off the names of those of us who had completed a card. In some instances he would read the name and ask the individual to please leave, in other instances he would read the name and ask the individual to take a seat in the front row. When he read my name he asked me to join the others in the front row. After reading all the names he said that those of us who had been asked to stay would be included in the group from which future contestants would be selected to be on the show. He further advised that those selected would be called within a few weeks.

Approximately 2 weeks later my wife received a call from "Password" asking if I could come to their offices at a specific time on a certain date. I did and I learned that they had assembled several teams from those of us selected at the show that would play the "Password" game against each other. The winner of each team would then be scheduled to play "Password" on a future television program.

Well, I came out as one of the winners and was a player on a television show that aired in February 1962. For those with short memories, Allen Ludden was the MC of the show, an absolutely marvelous host who put everyone at ease before the show even began. Betsy Palmer and Durward Kirby were the celebrities on the show and we had a BALL!! My opponent and I each played 2 games, one with Durward as our partner and the other with Betsy as our partner. It was such a beautiful experience!! Being with them was far more exciting than winning $700.00 and a Lucien Piccard wristwatch, my winnings for being on the show.

AEC-NASA SPACE NUCLEAR PROPULSION OFFICE

In October 1962, I was transferred back to AEC Headquarters in Germantown, Maryland as an administrative officer with the joint Atomic Energy Commission/National Aeronautics and Space Administration, Space Nuclear Propulsion Office. Harold Finger, a NASA employee, was the Director of the program and Milton Klein, an AEC employee, was the Deputy Director.

My primary responsibility was coordinating the industrial relations activities among our Space Nuclear Propulsion Offices in Germantown, Maryland; Cleveland, Ohio; Albuquerque, New Mexico and Las Vegas, Nevada. Our primary ground support contractor for our nuclear rocket testing site at Jackass Flats, Nevada was Pan American.

The objective of the program was the development of Nuclear Energy for Rocket Vehicle Application (NERVA) for deep space probes. The initial series of nuclear reactor tests for space application were conducted by the Los Alamos Scientific Laboratory (LASL) under the KIWI reactor program.

Suffice it to say that there was extensive research in reactor components and configuration, various propulsion concepts were studied, and a range of mission applications were evaluated prior to termination of the program in 1972.

TIME TO BUY A HOUSE

In January, 1962 I signed a contract for the construction of a 4 bedroom split foyer house to be built in the West end section of Rockville, Maryland later that year. Rockville was only 8 miles from the AEC Headquarters building in Germantown where I was working.

The price was $21,750 including central air conditioning and a wood-burning fireplace. The monthly mortgage payments were actually less than what I was then paying monthly for the apartment we were living in when we returned to Rockville from New York. I sold that same house in December 2000 for $240,000 and learned that in the spring of 2007 the buyer of my house sold it for $485,000.

We visited the house almost daily during its construction phase and went to settlement on the house in early September, 1963. A couple of our neighbors had already moved into their houses, including Dave and Margaret Baldridge who lived next door to us.

Dave was a Navy Captain with a PHD in Chemistry and a one-man team involved in developing a lethal shark bait for flyers and seamen who were forced to make emergency landings or abandon ship at sea. His subjects were rats; his goal was to develop and implant in rats a containerized combination of poisons that would be fatal to a shark when ingested, but would not kill the rat as sharks would attack only "live" bait.

He used to go to Bimini Islands for 4-6 weeks about 4 times a year to test his latest "death recipe" on the large population of sharks in that area. I think he finally abandoned the "don't kill the rat" scenario thinking he could tempt a hungry shark with a dead rat filled with poison. I understand that did not work either.

My wife and I went to Hollywood, Florida in June of 1965 where we joined Ray and Sophie Davis and their daughter Marsha. I had worked with Ray from the time I joined the Nuclear Rocket Program. Notwithstanding our difference in work locations, Ray in our Cleveland, Ohio Office and me in the Germantown, Maryland office, we developed a close friendship.

My goal while in Florida was to go deep sea fishing. I was able to join three other fisherman on a sport fishing charter boat out of Pompano Beach on the morning of June 17th. While trolling about a mile off-shore that afternoon, I hooked a 7 foot, 48 pound sailfish. It took about an hour, with bleeding blisters on both hands, before we got the sailfish in the boat. My dream had been realized as you might well imagine, one when we docked and the other when I hung the mounted fish over the fireplace on the wall in my recreation room.

GOT A HOUSE... WORKING ON A FAMILY!!

Once we settled into our new house, children to fill it became a top priority.

After almost a year with no results we decided to seek the assistance of a doctor. He suggested that Lilo be checked to make sure there were no blockage problems. Well, there were and the prognosis of her ever becoming pregnant was slim to impossible. She was devastated

The decision was simple...ADOPTION was the answer. Within a week or so we were meeting with a social worker from Catholic Charities at Saint Ann's Infants Home in D.C. We had several consultation sessions over the next several months, during which time we decided to have a son first and a daughter soon thereafter.

About 9 months later our social worker called to say they had selected a very handsome young man to be our son. He was born on September 5, 1965, and we carried him out of St. Ann's Infant Home in a suit on September 28th. We named him Glenn Joseph. Glenn after John Glenn who had orbited the earth about two years earlier, and Joseph, Lilo's only brother who had died in 1962 at age 39.

A month later, the 30th of October (Halloween), I received a call at my office from Catholic Charities requesting that I come to their offices that evening alone. The purpose of the meeting was to alert me to the fact that three of our neighbors had called Catholic Charities and reported that they had placed Glenn in an alcoholic home. The next morning I told Lilo of my meeting advising her that the social worker would be making unannounced visits to our home and if, in her opinion, she found any indication of excessive drinking action would be initiated to remove Glenn from our home. She was visibly shaken and assured me she would never drink again.

Our lives changed immediately. She stopped drinking. Her mother was living in Germany and accepted our invitation to come live with us. Glenn's adoption became final in September, 1966.

In January, 1969, we filed adoption papers with Catholic Charities to adopt a daughter. It was early April 1970 when they called and told us they had selected a beautiful young lady to be our daughter. She was born on March 5,1970. We walked out of St. Ann's Infants Home on April 12th with our beautiful daughter.

We had already named her Colleen Ann. and as with Glenn, all the neighbors were waiting outside when we drove into our driveway, waiting to see and hold our Colleen. It was just as exciting that day as the day we brought Glenn home 4 and a half years earlier. What a beautiful family we had!

Lilo began drinking again within a year following Colleen's adoption. In an effort to help her and improve our quality of life, I went to court and got a court order to have her committed for 96 hours (the maximum time allowed) in a local hospital detoxification ward. When she was discharged I had already enrolled her in a recovery program at the same hospital, but it lasted less than a week.

A local priest who was a recovering alcoholic visited her daily at our home and tried to get her to join him at AA meetings, prayed with her, etc. but to no avail. Everything got progressively worse and after several years with brief periods of sobriety and extended periods of abuse, embarrassment and many, many days and nights of sheer hell, Lilo died in her sleep during the night of June 15, 1979 from acute, chronic alcoholism. It was a blessing for her and our family.

Lilo's mom, "Oma" stayed with us until her death in May of 1983 at the age of 87 and is buried next to her daughter at the Gate of Heaven Cemetery in Silver Springs, MD.

REPORT TO THE GENERAL MANAGER'S OFFICE!!

In 1966 I was transferred to the General Manager's Office to work with the former General Counsel of the AEC on a Federal-State cooperative program to upgrade state workmen's compensation laws. This program was initiated by AEC Commissioner, Jim Ramey, to provide adequate workmen's compensation coverage for individuals working in radiation environments, especially in states where the AEC had large contractor operated facilities.

Many of the state laws required that a workmen's compensation claim must be filed within some specified period of time, usually 2 to 5 years from the date of the onset of a radiation related disease/disability, employee's retirement or termination of employment. Because of the latent nature of radiation induced diseases, the final date for the filing of a claim may have expired years before the disease or condition manifested in the radiation worker.

Because of the large number of radiation workers employed by AEC contractors throughout the United States, the AEC felt an obligation to work with those states with limited benefits to amend their workmen's compensation laws to meet certain minimum standards necessary to afford adequate protection to the radiation worker population.

I was assigned to work with the Governors and their staffs in

13 western states, I worked primarily with the state industrial commissioners, reviewing with them our analysis of their state's workmen's compensation law and offering any assistance they might need in securing an amendment to their laws that would incorporate our minimum standards.

Most states were cooperative. New Mexico, however, with the large number of radiation workers employed at one of the largest AEC owned facilities, the Los Alamos Scientific Laboratory in Santa Fe, did not want the Federal government messing in their business.

My contact in New Mexico was Ricardo Montoya, Chairman of the State Industrial Commission at that time and fully supportive of our program. Following several meetings with Montoya and members of the state legislature, he called me one afternoon and asked if I could possibly come to Santa Fe to brief members of the State Legislature on our program at 1:00 PM the next day. He agreed to meet my plane in Albuquerque and drive me to Santa Fe. Everything was a go!

I got an early flight the next morning and Montoya met me in Albuquerque. At 1:00 PM that afternoon he was introducing me to the state legislature. While he was introducing me a gentlemen handed me a handwritten note that read, "Get the hell out of this state and don't come back." It was signed Jack Campbell, Governor. I showed the note to Montoya when he returned to his seat. He read it and returned to the podium and announced that I would be unable to address them as planned.

I returned to Montoya's office with him and called Jim Ramey, the AEC Commissioner considered the "father" of the program. He instructed me to ignore the Governor's order and spend the next couple of days walking conspicuously around the capital grounds and in the Capitol, which I did. Nobody approached me and I returned to Washington two days later. The New Mexico State Legislature still had not amended their workmen's compensation law when the program ended in 1974.

ENTER ENERGY RESEARCH AND DEVELOPMENT ADMINISTRATION

In December, 1974, the AEC was absorbed into the newly created "Energy Research and Development Administration" (ERDA). Bob Seamans, formerly the Administrator of the National Aeronautics and Space Administration, was appointed Administrator

When I first learned that this organizational change was underway, I contacted the Director of Human Resources and expressed my desire to join the Congressional Affairs staff at the Energy Research and Development Administration (ERDA). Word came back that a Hollister (Holly) Cantus had been selected by Seamans to become the Director of Congressional Affairs at ERDA.

Within a week or two I got a call from Holly saying that he had heard I was interested in joining his Congressional Affairs staff. I told him I was and we set up a time to get together. At that time Holly was working in the Department of Defense (DOD) Congressional Affairs Office located in the Pentagon.

I was very impressed and pleased with Holly's demeanor. He was very personable and had a great sense of humor. He also told me he was looking for an Assistant Director for Research and

Administration in his ERDA office and advised me that my competition for the position was a female army colonel who was on his DOD staff.

About 2 or 3 weeks later I received a call from Holly…His opening remark was, "Are you ready to go to work?" My immediate response "You bet I am!" During the next 2-3 weeks we discussed what I would be responsible for, the staff needed to do the job, etc. I ended up with 6 professional and 2 clerical staff positions with an overall total of approximately 35 positions in the Congressional Affairs Office.

Holly put together a GREAT staff who were personable, helpful and cooperative. We were a fine team with an outstanding leader!

I thought I knew my way around the government pretty well when I was hired into this job, however, I had a lot to learn. I had no experience in dealing with the egos and constituent problems of 100 Senators and 435 House Members. It was a sink or swim situation and I was a swimmer! Holly would often stop by my office during the day to encourage and guide me in some situations that we dared not "screw-up." The potential consequences were just too gruesome to think about, but one day it happened!

I received a phone call early one morning and my secretary came back to my desk to tell me it was Congressman John Murtha from Pennsylvania on the phone. I picked up the phone with a cheery "Good morning, Mr. Congressman." He returned the greeting and asked if I could come over to his office right away saying it was important and he needed to talk with me. I told him I certainly could and left immediately…it was about an 8 minute walk to his office building but it only took me 4 that morning!

His receptionist did not even know me, yet asked if I was Mr. Kneeland. (bad sign…he wanted to make sure I was directed to his office as soon as I arrived) I assured her I was and she escorted me into his office. The congressman shook my hand, introduced me to his staff assistant, and invited me to sit down. I still did not have a clue why he wanted to see me, but I was about to find out.

He started by saying that he was terribly embarrassed. He had read the morning paper from his District in Pennsylvania and learned that ERDA had awarded a multi-million dollar contract for research to address problems associated with methane gas in coal mines. He then asked me if I thought that he might have had some interest in knowing about the contract before it was awarded rather then reading about it in the morning paper in the form of an announcement by a Pennsylvania senator. OH SHIT…THIS WAS SERIOUS!! I immediately recalled that I had notified both senators, but not Congressman Murtha. A major oversight on my part and inconsistent with established protocol in making congressional notifications on major contract awards. Murtha should have received advance notice of the pending contract award 24 hours prior to any notice to senators, or any other congressman in the state or the news media.

I apologized for this serious violation of protocol and accepted full responsibility for the error.

I was expecting him to advise me that he would be bringing this matter to the attention of Holly or even the Administrator for whatever action he might deem appropriate (firing was most common in these situations). Instead, he commented to the effect that he was sure I would not overlook his interest in any ERDA activities in the future that might be carried out in his District or in the State of Pennsylvania.

I assured him that his interests would be foremost in my mind with regard to any ERDA programs or activities planned or executed in the State of Pennsylvania. With that he shook my hand and assured me that everything we had discussed in his office would stay in his office. I expressed my sincere appreciation for his understanding and reassured him that it would not be repeated.

Notwithstanding this most serious blunder, my career with the Energy Research and Development Administration organization was very exciting and challenging and I thoroughly enjoyed working with Holly and our office staff.

U.S. DEPARTMENT OF ENERGY ACTIVATED ON OCTOBER 1, 1977

The Department of Energy (D0E) was created on August 4, 1977, and activated 2 months later on October 1, 1977, with Secretary James Schlesinger at the helm. ERDA was absorbed into the new Energy Department.

Secretary Schlesinger selected Fred Hitz to be his Assistant for Congressional Affairs in the Department of Energy. Paul Cyr, a World War II hero, was appointed as Fred's deputy.

Following several months of "organizational shake-down" my position as a Program Liaison Director was established. In this position I was the principal point of contact between the Congress and Department of Energy management officials, including the Assistant Secretary for Management and Administration, Assistant Secretary for Environment, Safety and Health, Administrator for the Economic Regulatory Administration, the Director of the Office of Policy, Planning and Analysis and the General Council.among others.

Maintaining daily contact with the above identified individuals and their staff was essential in keeping Members of Congress current on specific legislative initiatives and issues of critical importance in support of Administration objectives. My advice and that of my staff was sought and relied upon by these officials in assessing the legislative implications and political impacts of major policy and program proposals.

This daily contact was not only essential in day-to-day coordination of activities between the Department of Energy and the Congress, but also in assisting individual Representatives, Senators and their staffs in responding to issues of importance to their constituents as well as the staff and Members of committees of jurisdiction in both the US House of Representatives and the U.S. Senate.

In March 1981 the President appointed Bill Heffelfinger to be the Assistant Secretary of Energy for Administration. Cyr informed me that I would, in addition to my other duties, be Bill Heffelfinger's personal congressional affairs person. I had never met the man, but was told he weighed about 400 pounds and had the reputation of being the hardest man in the world to work for or work with.

I called Bill and told him I would be his congressional affairs person and would welcome the opportunity to meet him at his convenience. His response was "lets do it right now"!! We met for over an hour during which time he made it very clear that if asked he would be willing to meet with members of Congress or testify at congressional committee hearings. (He would really have had no choice in such matters.) However, he did ask me to do whatever I could to keep him off the Hill as much as possible. I had no problem with that.

A few months after being confirmed by the Senate as the Assistant Secretary for Administration, Bill was invited to testify at an oversight hearing before the House Energy and Commerce Committee, chaired by Congressman John Dingell from the state of Michigan.

I accompanied Bill to the hearing and was surprised when only the Chairman and one other member of the committee were present from a committee that numbered over 50 members. I was looking for more committee members to show up at any time, especially Congressman Bud Brown, a Republican from Ohio who was the Ranking Minority Member on the Committee.

My worst fears were realized when the Committee Chairman asked Heffelfinger to please stand and raise his right hand to be sworn in as he wanted his testimony to be under oath. After swearing him in the Chairman referenced a document that had been brought to his attention in which Heffelfinger had claimed to have received the "William Jump Memorial Foundation Award"a very prestigious performance award for civilian career employees in the Federal Government. Heffelfinger denied having ever made such a statement. However, he did state that he had been nominated for the award but never received or claimed to have received the award.

At this point I left the hearing room and went to Congressman Browns' office to get some support for Heffelfinger. He was out, but his secretary got him on the phone for me. I explained that the Committee Chairman had placed Heffelfinger under oath and was challenging his integrity and honesty regarding his testimony. Bud advised that he was on his way . I went back to the hearing room and Bud came in right behind me. He asked the Chairman if he had changed the subject of the hearing without informing him, reminding the Chairman that he was the Ranking Minority Member of the Committee. I do not recall exactly what the Chairman's response was, but the hearing came to a close shortly after Congressman Brown's appearance and the subject of the award was never raised again to my knowledge. I understand that the Chairman apologized to Heffelfinger for challenging his honesty and integrity.

Heffelfinger credited me with saving his life on several occasions during hearings before House and Senate Committees of jurisdiction and subsequently told the Secretary of Energy that "Kneeland walks on water." I had a friend for life so long as Heffelfinger was alive. He rewarded me with a free parking space in our building where I worked, plus he had my name added to the list of DOE staff authorized to use the department's limousine service.

About a year later Heffelfinger suffered a fatal heart attack on a Sunday in his kitchen. The minute I walked into his office that Monday morning I knew he had died. Everyone in sight was crying...they all loved him.

SIX MONTH WHITE HOUSE ASSIGNMENT

During the spring of 1978, I received a 6 month assignment to work in the White House to assist President Carter's efforts in minimizing the potential for proliferation of highly enriched uranium. The President's approach was to invite the leadership of the House and Senate committees of jurisdiction to the White House for a briefing on the positive effects termination of the Clinch River Breeder Reactor Program would have in substantially reducing the availability, hence proliferation, of highly enriched uranium.

It was my responsibility to contact the appropriate congressional committees having programmatic or oversight responsibilities over Department of Energy programs and invite their chairmen, members, and staff to the White House for a briefing on the President's proposal. I scheduled daily briefings to accommodate the schedules of the congressional leadership and the personal and committee staff of Members of both the U.S. Senate and House of Representatives. John Deutch. Undersecretary of the Department of Energy at the time, conducted the briefings.

Notwithstanding the number of briefings conducted over the 6 month period, the Congress did not take the legislative action necessary to terminate the Clinch River Breeder Reactor Program until 1983.

During the Reagan Administration I met and worked with his White House congressional staff on many occasions involving both Administration and Congressional issues, but termination of the Clinch River Breeder Reactor Program was not among them.

In November, 1982, the President appointed Donald Hodel to be the Secretary of Energy. In February 1985 President Reagan appointed Donald Hodel to become the Secretary of the Department of Interior and appointed John Herrington to replace Hodel as Secretary of Energy. Secretary Herrington appointed Ted Garrish to be his Assistant Secretary for Congressional, Intergovernmental and Public Affairs. My responibilities remained basically the same under Ted as they were under his predecessor, Rob Odel, who was the Assistant Secretary for Congressional Affairs under Secretary Hodel.

When Ted took over, I had in place a cooperative arrangement with congressional staff in the committees of jurisdiction in both the House and Senate regarding Secretarial hearings before their committees. Specifically, if I delivered the Secretary's prepared testimony to them 48 hours prior to Committee/subcommittee hearings, they would provide me, 24 hours prior to the hearing, a copy of the questions prepared by their committee staff for their members use in asking questions of the Secretary during the hearing. In other words, the Secretary would know in advance most of the questions he would be expected to be asked during the hearing.

To make sure we didn't miss any questions that might be raised by a member, but were not included in questions prepared by the committee staff, my staff contacted the energy legislative assistant of each committee member to be sure we knew of any specific questions the member planned to raise with the Secretary during the subject hearing. In other words, I had the Secretary covered on all bases.

If, based upon a review of information received from our canvassing efforts, it was determined that a briefing session with the Secretary was appropriate in preparing him to be responsive to issues likely to be raised during the hearing, Rob Odle and I would then arrange for such a briefing, including participation by appropriate program Assistant Secretaries responsible for program matters that we anticipated might be raised during the hearing.

I informed Ted of this arrangement and asked if he would want me to continue the practice with Secretary Herrington. He advised that he would handle all congressional matters for Secretary Herrington.

Although I had not given any serious thought to retirement, I knew it was time to retire when, during a return trip to the office in the Secretary's limousine with the Secretary and Ted following a hearing before the Senate Energy Committee, both expressed the view that I had let the Secretary be "blind-sided" by not alerting them to issues raised during the hearing.

When we got back to the office I gave Ted my notice that I would be retiring effective two weeks from that day, November 9, 1987. I also told him that I did not want a retirement party at the Fort McNair Officers' Club, a standard practice when employees with a long tenure in positions comparable to mine retired from the Department.

I regret having made that decision as there were a lot of close friends who had wanted the opportunity to personally acknowledge my 32 years of Federal service and to wish me well in my retirement.

However, Shirley deJavanne of my office staff was not about to let me leave without proper "fan-fare." She put together a

GREAT party at a downtown hotel that included many close and dear friends throughout the Department…it began about noon and continued well into the evening! What a Party…I will never forget it!! THANKS SHIRLEY!!

Bill Martin, Deputy Secretary of the Department, invited me to his office on my last day to express his appreciation for my services on the Hill. I enjoyed working with Bill on a number of sensitive issues involving the Department, the White House and the Congress during my last years with the Department.

I retired on November 23rd, 1987 with a total of 33 years of Federal Service, including 4 years in the Military and one year of compensatory service for 14 months of unused sick leave.

AND THEN I FLUNKED RETIREMENT

After a few months of painting and wallpapering my house, I decided it was time to go back to work. Darleen Earhart, a former neighbor, ladyfriend, and whom I became engaged to in August 1980, returned to Ohio in 1985 where she and her deceased husband had lived before moving to Pennsylvania and then to Rockville, Maryland in 1974.

After commuting between Rockville, Maryland and Waverly, Ohio, about every other week for about 2 years, I contacted Congressman Bob McEwen who represented Southern Ohio and asked if he would contact the management at the Department of Energy uranium enrichment plant in Piketon regarding employment opportunities.

He did, and I received a call from Ralph Donnelly, then Manager of the plant, a few weeks later, inviting me to come in for an interview. Our interview went well and I began working in the Public Affairs Office at the plant on May 8, 1988.

I was able to rent an apartment in Waverly about 5 miles from the plant and 4 miles from where Darleen lived on Lake White. Everything was going my way!!!!

After working in Public Affairs for a year, Ralph Donnelly called me into his office and asked if I would like a job as his

Executive Assistant. I jumped at it. In that position I was also a member of the plant management committee which included the managers of the various divisions in the plant, the financial officer, security, etc.

In 1990 I received the Martin Marietta Energy Systems Management Achievement Award which was presented during Awards Night in Oak Ridge, Tennessee, in September 1990.

I thoroughly enjoyed working with Ralph and being a part of the plant's management team up until the time Ralph transferred back to Oak Ridge, Tennessee and Dale Allen from Oak Ridge became the plant manager.

I retired from the United States Enrichment Corporation, successor to Martin Marietta Corporation as operator of the DOE Enrichment Plant in July 1997.

TED STRICKLAND, A FRIEND AND GOVERNOR

In 1991 Ted Strickland entered the race for his first term as Congressman from Southern Ohio. His district included Piketon, Ohio, location of the Department of Energy uranium enrichment plant where I worked. After learning he was running for Congress, I invited him to visit the plant and meet our 5,000 employees who lived in the surrounding area. He accepted and our friendship began. I thoroughly enjoyed our friendship and the occasional dinners I shared with him and his wife Frances at the Emmit House restaurant in Waverly. Ted won the election for his first term to Congress.

It was not long before Frank Cremeans announced he was going to run against Ted in the next election. His money got him elected.

Ted did not wait long to make it known that he would be running for the seat he had lost to Cremeans in the next election. Ted won the next election overwhelmingly and continued serving in Congress for a total of 12 years. He withdrew his candidacy for Congressman in 2006 and ran for Governor of Ohio. He won handily.

At Ted's invitation, Donna and I joined the Governor's Circle of Friends and attended the Governor's Celebration Reception on November 16, 2007, in Columbus. We thoroughly enjoyed the opportunity to chat briefly with him and Frances during the reception. He's a GREAT GUY and is proving to be an OUTSTANDING GOVERNOR.

BECOMING A BUILDING BRIDGES VOLUNTEER

In February, 2001, I became a part-time volunteer with the "Building Bridges" program, established by the Montgomery County Ohio Juvenile Court System. I was a mentor, tutor and counselor to juveniles between the ages of 12 and 18 who were on probation for various crimes including drug abuse, assault, auto theft, larceny, criminal mischief, etc. Tim Poulos was the probation officer for the juvenile group with whom I worked.

Many of the juveniles had never graduated from an elementary school and lived with only one parent, or a more distant relative (an older sibling, an aunt, etc) For many, exposure to drugs, violence, and alcohol was part of their daily life.

My weekly highlight was taking 4-6 of the group to the Dayton Veterans Hospital on Wednesday evenings to assist handicapped veterans play bingo. The kids loved it (it made them feel needed) and so did the veterans. All winnings went to the vets although many of them were very willing to give or share their winnings with their helper. However, to assure uniformity and fairness to all we insisted that the veterans keep their winnings.

I thoroughly enjoyed my time with the Building Bridges Program. I experienced some successes in counseling and working with many of the participants, but also some disappointments.

I worked with the Building Bridges approximately 3 years before joining the Avis Car Rental Agency driving rental cars between the Dayton International Airport and Avis rental agencies within the Dayton area and in neighboring states.

OPEN HEART SURGERY

My part time employment driving Avis rental cars came to an abrupt end about 6:30 AM on Tuesday, March 28, 2006, when I experienced a brief dizzy spell while preparing to go to work. Ironically, Donna, my significant other, witnessed my careening backwards across the kitchen floor. I sat down for a couple minutes, felt fine and got up to leave for work. Ms Donna would not hear of it and called 911 to request an ambulance to take me to Miami Valley Hospital.

Upon my arrival at the hospital, I underwent a series of tests, scans, etc. My cardiologist at the time advised that there was some blockage in my heart vessels and a small leak in the mitral valve. He opined that the blockages could probably be corrected by angioplasty or stents and that the mitral valve leak was small.

At the request of Dr. Joffe, from whom I had requested a second opinion, I obtained the original tape of the CAT scan. Upon viewing the tape he determined that there were blockages and a leaking mitral valve. Having been told that Dr Joffe was not taking on new patients, I asked him if I was now his patient...he said I was! I was admitted to the Dayton Heart Hospital on April 5th where he did a heart catherization which determined that stents were not an option due to the extent of my blockages. A quadruple bypass and repair or replacement of my mitral valve was the Order of the Day!

I was scheduled for open heart surgery late on the morning of April 7th. I called Colleen, my daughter in Maryland, to advise her of my date with the surgeon. She immediately gathered her family together and Phil, her husband, drove her and their 2 children to Dayton that night, arriving in Dayton about 3:00 AM. After a short nap Colleen joined Donna who was already at the hospital.

I was taken into surgery about noon on the 7th. I have been told that my cardiac surgeon came out of surgery about 10:30 PM that evening to tell Donna and Colleen, who had been waiting outside the operating room, that I was not responding well. He told them that he could not get the blood count up (it was 7) after 6 units of blood had been administered. He told Donna and Colleen that he had checked, double checked and tripled checked what could be causing this problem. However, it soon became obvious that blood was filling the tissue in the neck area as evidenced by swelling and discoloration of the neck. He immediately removed the shunt from the neck area and placed one in my arm. After administering 2 more units of blood, the blood count began to rise and everyone sighed a breath of relief! I received a total of 8 units of blood.

The surgeon also explained to Donna and Colleen that he had attempted to repair the mitral valve. However, following the repair he discovered that it was still leaking and the chest had to be reopened and the valve had to be replaced with a new valve made from pig tissue. Only after the blood count began to rise did my surgeon go home to get some much deserved rest! Because of the critically low blood count following surgery, 2 brain scans were taken to confirm that I had not suffered a stroke. A pacemaker was also implanted the next day, April 8th.

I have no recollection of anything that happened during the

next 10 days that I spent in the Intensive Care Unit, with my arms and legs tethered to the bed for my own safety because of the plugging of tubes and my removal of the catherer. Donna and Colleen watched me struggling for 10 days to free myself from the tethers and being fed through a tube in my nose.

Following my discharge from the hospital, I learned from a University of California Los Angeles (UCLA) medical publication that I was experiencing "postoperative delirium." The report, entitled "Anesthesia and Your Brain, noted that General anesthesia can lead to postoperative delirium in some older adults." The article went on to state that "disturbing reports have suggested that some older adults who receive general anesthesia have a notable decline in their mental (cognitive) function for 2 years after certain surgeries. The condition is called postoperative cognitive dysfunction. The report goes on to say, "Choice of anesthesia drugs may adversely affect the postoperative outcome." You can bet I will be checking this out should I ever need surgery again!

I remained in a very confused and delirious state until the day before I was discharged on April 18th from the ICU and the hospital. Dr. Joffe had wanted to place me in a hospital adjacent to the Dayton Heart Hospital for 2 weeks of rehabilitation before coming home. Donna and Colleen met with Dr. Joffe to discuss home therapy instead since there were no stairs to climb and being home would expedite my recovery process.

A nurse and a physical therapist came to the home frequently for about 2 weeks. Then I was enrolled in an 8 week physical therapy program at the Samaritan North Rehab Center. Weekly progress in my strength and mental alertness was obvious to all.

Following 8 weeks of therapy at Samaritan North rehab center, I joined the YMCA center in Englewood where I have continued my physical therapy 3 days per week which I plan to continue indefinitely.

Before closing I want to thank my former secretary, Linda Shoemaker, for her persistence in arranging for me to meet her widowed sister, Donna. We have been sharing our lives together for the last 12 years and look forward to many more years of love and companionship together!! **THANKS LINDA!**

In closing I want to remember my parents.

ALASKAN CRUISE MAY/JUNE 2007

On May 22, 2007, Donna and I, her sister Phyllis and husband Paul and her sister Linda and her husband John, departed the safety of our homes and ventured into the pristine wilderness of Alaska on a 13 day cruise aboard the PRINCESS LINE. The fun began immediately!

Upon our arrival in Anchorage we spent the first night in the Hotel Captain Cook in Anchorage. The next day (5/23) we traveled by rail to Talkeetna where we boarded a bus to MT. MCKINLEY PRINCESS WILDERNESS LODGE. The next day (5/24) we departed Talkeetna by rail to the DENALI PRINCESS WILDERNESS LODGE where we would spend 2 nights.

The next morning we boarded a bus that would take us on a tour of Denali Park, the highlight of our trip. The first wildlife we saw upon entering the park was a moose with 2 young calves. Our second sighting was a pair of grizzly bears "on the hunt." I say on the hunt as we learned from our guide that grizzlies are always looking for their next meal. Since they were in relative close proximity to the moose calves, (only a few 1000 yards apart on the same mountain range) I could not help but sense the danger confronting the 2 young calves, and perhaps their mother as well.

The next day, while walking back to the hotel after souvenir shopping with Paul and John, we suddenly noticed a cow moose grazing along the edge of a busy highway within 8-10 feet of the path we were on. She was ignoring us as well as the traffic backup she was creating along the highway.

Our cruise ship stopped at a few cities enroute to our final destination including Juneau where we boarded a cable car for a short ride to the top of a mountain overlooking Juneau, the capital city of Alaska. While there we saw a bald eagle that had been shot and was being cared for in a protective shelter as he was unable to fly without hitting obstructions in his flight path.

Our next stop was in Ketchikan where we boarded a bus that took us to a lake where we were able to see a crab trap submerged in the lake. Upon our return to where we boarded the boat, we were taken into a dining room and served one of the finest "crab feasts" I have ever had.

Following lunch we returned to Ketchikan where we boarded our cruise ship that took us into Glacier Bay. After spending several hours enroute to Glacier Bay, we spent several hours viewing the glacier and the chunks of ice that fell from the glacier into the bay.

After leaving Glacier Bay we spent 2-3 days enroute to our final cruise destination, VanCouver, British Columbia. We spent a full day and a night relishing the highlights of VanCouver, much of it on foot and a horse drawn carriage.

We departed VanCouver early on the morning of June 3rd for a flight to Minneapolis and then onto Dayton International Airport. The memories of the trip and the superb services and recreational activities offered aboard the cruise ship will be with us foreverl...IT WAS GREAT!

FEBRUARY 2009...HAWAII BOUND

Donna, her 2 sisters, Phyllis and Linda, and their spouses and I spent 10 days on the beautiful island of Oahu. The first day was spent taking in the history and events of the Japanese attack on Pearl Harbor on December 7, 1941, including the Pearl Harbor Memorial, ships at anchor in the Bay including the USS Missouri on which the Declaration of Surrender was signed by General McArthur for the United States and Premier Tojo for the Japanese.

Our tour guide went out of his way to show us the many points of interest including the National Cemetery for many of the casualties resulting from the attack on December 7, 1941, and the apartment building where President Obama was raised during part of his childhood.

A tour of the Dole pineapple plantation, hiking up mountain trails to view the ocean below, and strolling the beautiful sandy beaches adjacent to our rented condo filled our vacation with excitement and relaxation. The photos reflect the beauty and excitement of our visit far better than I can describe:

A REUNION OF THE WINDHAM HIGH SCHOOL CLASS of 1950

Following my Hawaiian vacation, coupled with the bitter cold of a lingering winter, I made a decision to undertake the coordination of a reunion of my High School Class of 1950 from Windham High School. The fact that I was not able to attend two previous reunions held in 1975 and 1990 was a strong incentive for me to undertake this effort. After a few phone calls to classmates whom I had contacted once or twice during the intervening 59 years assured me this was the thing to do.

With a 2008 update of the Windham High School Alumni Directory, I began searching for graduates in the class of 1950. I was told that there were 243 graduates in our class.

The Directory provided the name, address and phone number for those alumni who had submitted, at some time since graduation, information for inclusion in the Directory, including the married name of many classmates. Regretably, however, there was NO updated information on over fifty percent of the class. I was able to gather information on 144 classmates, but was unable to validate that the addresses were correct.

Roberta Marmo, a Florida resident, learned about my reunion plans. She had assisted in contacting classmates for the 1990 reunion and offered to send me the list of 1950 graduates that they used in contacting classmates for the 1950 reunion. I compared her list with mine and found the names and addresses of an additional 40 classmates that were on her list but not on mine.

With this information I sent an April 1 letter to a total of 184 addressees advising them of my intention to coordinate a class reunion on June 20 at the Nathan Hale Inn and Convention center on the Uconn campus. Over 60 of these letters were returned for various reasons, primarily "No forwarding address."

After checking with a number of graduates I ended up with a list of 128 classmates, of whom 39 responded that they would attend and would be accompanied by 21 guests, for a total of 60. On the day of the reunion 2 of the 39 classmates who advised they would be attending did not show.

In conclusion, I thoroughly enjoyed coordinating the reunion and those attending expressed their delight and appreciation for putting together the PERFECT reunion. My reward and that of our alumni is that we are having another reunion on June 26, 2010, starting at 3:00 PM, in the same place, THE NATHAN HALE INN AND CONVENTION CENTER on the Uconn Campus at Storrs, Connecticut.

Bring on the world

This was our cruise ship, the U.S.N.S. General M.B. Stewart, that would take us to Bremerhaven, during the next 11 days.

University of Vienna - Institute of Criminology

CERTIFICATE

This is to certify that

Mr. Harold E. Kneeland

has successfully completed the special course in

Psychology of Criminal Interrogation

and

Scientific Criminal Investigation

as prepared by the Institute of Criminology at the

UNIVERSITY OF VIENNA.

Given under my hand and seal

this 18 th day of September 1953 at Vienna, Austria.

Roland Graßberger

Dr. Roland E. Graßberger
DIRECTOR OF THE INSTITUTE
PROFESSOR OF CRIMINAL LAW AND
CRIMINOLOGY, UNIVERSITY OF VIENNA

DEPARTMENT OF THE ARMY

THIS IS TO CERTIFY THAT
THE SECRETARY OF THE ARMY HAS AWARDED

THE COMMENDATION RIBBON

WITH METAL PENDANT

TO

Corporal Harold E. Kneeland,

RA 11 217 832, MILITARY POLICE CORPS

FOR

MERITORIOUS SERVICE PERFORMED AT AUGSBURG, GERMANY DURING
THE PERIOD 7 JULY 1952 TO 30 NOVEMBER 1953

GIVEN UNDER MY HAND IN THE CITY OF WASHINGTON
THIS 15TH DAY OF DECEMBER 1953

Lt. Colonel Roy Marcy, Commanding Officer Augsburg Military Detachment, pinning the award medal on my uniform

AUGSBURG DETACHMENT
APO 178 US ARMY

5. Feb. 1954

SAMAU-CO 201.2

SUBJECT: Commendation

THRU: Commanding Officer,
Co "C", 793d MP Bn
APO 178, US Army

TO: Cpl Harold E Kneeland, RA11217832,
13th CID
APO 178, US Army

1. It has been officially brought to my attention that your efforts and attention to duty contributed directly to the apprehension of suspects in two different rape cases on the night of 25 January 1954. Facts reveal that in conjunction with other patrolmen these suspects were apprehended within a period of four (4) hours.

2. As an investigator in these cases you showed unusual initiative and devotion to duty in bringing about the expeditious closing of these cases. You are commended for the performance of outstanding duty and initiative in assisting in the apprehension of suspects in such a short period of time. In view of the fact that initially there were no leads your endeavors are particularly noteworthy in that your efforts generated enthusiasm among the other investigators and patrolmen which resulted in the discovery of leads that brought suspects under direct surveillance that led to their apprehension.

3. Superior performance of duty such as this is indicative of a great sense of responsibility, interest, and a high degree of professional knowledge in your assigned duties.

4. A copy of this letter will be placed in your official 201 file.

Roy W. Marcy

ROY W. MARCY
Lt Colonel, Infantry
Commanding

Tel: Augs Mil 8306

Wedding breakfast

Honorable Discharge

from the Armed Forces of the United States of America

This is to certify that

HAROLD EUGENE KNEELAND RA 11 217 832 CORPORAL REGULAR ARMY

was Honorably Discharged from the

Army of the United States

on the 30 TH day of DECEMBER 1954 This certificate is awarded as a testimonial of Honest and Faithful Service

ROSCOE H. GODDEN
Major QMC

PERIOD of MILITARY SERVICE
January 15, 1951 – December 30, 1954

Our home during my college years

Mansfield VFW Commander Is Sophomore Uconn Vet

The future criminals of America had best beware, for Harold] Kneeland is preparing to cope with them. A fourth semester studei who has gov't, English accounting and psychology courses as the mai body of his curriculum, he is a pre-law major who has something ‹ a unique background.

At the present time Harold is commander of the Veterans of Foreig Wars post in Mansfield.

Harold is a veteran who spent four years with the Army in Ge: many. Here he was attached to the Criminal Investigation Divisioi Since he had been an honor student at both the Army Military Polic and Criminal Investigation ser ice schools, he was one of thirtee men in Europe at the time to l selected to attend the University ‹ Vienna.

Campus Photo—Jacobson

Harold Kneeland

At the university he studie criminology and was well on tl way to becoming a homicide e: pert. He received the Army Con mendation Medal which requir the approval of a major general. A the time he received his positio as criminal investgator, he wa the youngest one accredited by tl Army.

A native of Storrs he spenc his spare time hunting, fishin and skiing but still keeping an ey on the developments in the fiel of criminology. Married for tw years, he and his wife, a Germa National, went back to German this summer to visit her relative:

The University of Connecticut

To all to whom these presents may come greeting
Be it known that

Harold Eugene Kneeland

having satisfied the requirements for the Degree of

Master of Arts

in the

Graduate School

has been admitted to that degree with all the
honors, privileges, and obligations thereto appertaining
In Testimony Whereof the seal of the University and the signatures
as authorized by the Board of Trustees are hereunto affixed
Given at Storrs on the twelfth day of June, A.D., 1960

Abraham Ribicoff
PRESIDENT OF THE BOARD OF TRUSTEES

N. L. Whetten
DEAN

A. N. Jorgensen
PRESIDENT OF THE UNIVERSITY

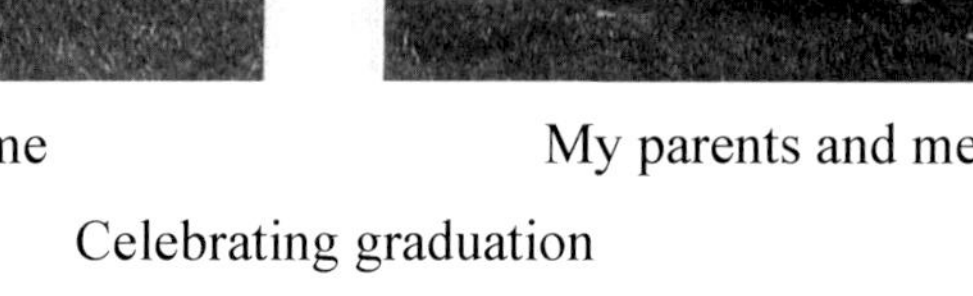

Lilo and me

My parents and me

Celebrating graduation

My fishing trophy

My children's growing years

Mom and Dad's Golden Wedding Anniversary, April, 1982